THE PRACTICAL EPISTLE OF JAMES

Studies in Applied Christianity

THE PRACTICAL EPISTLE OF JAMES

Studies in Applied Christianity

---

by FRANK E. GAEBELEIN
Headmaster, The Stony Brook School

DONIGER & RAUGHLEY, INC.
Great Neck, New York

Library of Congress Catalog Card No.: 55-7558
Printed in the U. S. A.
By The Haddon Craftsmen, Inc.

PREFACE

THIS BOOK CONTAINS the substance of a series of lectures on the Epistle of James, delivered before the Convention Chrétienne of Morges, Switzerland, in September 1952, as well as at a number of churches and conferences in America, including the Old First Presbyterian Church of Orange, New Jersey, Calvary Baptist Church of New York, and "The Firs," Bellingham, Washington. It was at the suggestion of Professor J. M. Nicole of the Institut Biblique, Nogent-s.-Marne, France, who interpreted for the author at Morges, that the lectures were written out for translation into French and for publication, first in *Mission,* the periodical of the Groupes Missionaires of Switzerland, France, and Belgium, and later as a small book, entitled *L'Épitre de Jacques.* During 1953-54, they were also serialized in the Bible Study magazine, *Our Hope.*

As the reader will see, these lectures are neither an exhaustive study nor a technical commentary. Their aim is simply to present the incisive ethical and spiritual teaching that makes the Epistle of James such a vividly practical portion of the New Testament. For it is the author's conviction that the message of the plain-spoken brother of our Lord Jesus Christ is one that is urgently needed by the Church today.

FRANK E. GAEBELEIN

Stony Brook, Long Island
Christmas, 1954

CONTENTS

INTRODUCTION

Among the New Testament writings, the Epistle of James has had perhaps less justice done it than almost any other. Commentaries upon it are rather few in number, compared with those on the other epistles of similar length. And the significant fact is that James has been neglected and misunderstood not so much by those of liberal theological views as by evangelicals, and even fundamentalists.

This is the letter that Martin Luther so cordially disliked, even to the extent of calling it "a right strawy epistle." And while we know that the reformer was in this instance quite wrong, we should, in humility and with proper respect for this great man of God, endeavor to understand something of the reason for his error. Engaged as he was in a tremendous battle against a corrupt church, and used by God to recover for the Lord's people the central doctrine of justification by faith, he thought that James, in his emphasis upon works at the end of his second chapter, contradicted Paul's teaching of justification by faith.

With us it is different. Today most informed Bible students know, as we shall see in detail later in our exposition, that on the question of faith and works James and Paul are supplementary; they complement, not contradict, one another.

Yet the epistle is still neglected. There are those who say that it is "only elementary" in its teaching. They tell us that it is "for the Jews," not for us. It contains, they say, "no Gospel." And it is, they assert, "merely legalistic" and so has comparatively little to give those who know what it means to be not under law but under grace.

What shall we say to such an attitude toward the Epistle of James? Simply this: we may say that the New Testament is full of the moral and ethical and social challenge of the Christian faith. The Bible does have something to say about such things as liberty, justice, and personal righteousness. It speaks in thunderous tones about social abuses. In a day when Christians are longing and praying for revival, we need to remember that an essential prelude to revival is a renewed sensitiveness to sin in the individual life and in the Christian community. Much of what James says may be "elementary" from the doctrinal point of view, yet from the practical point of view it is far advanced. These are days when we need to get back to the plain, practical things about which he speaks with such forthright boldness.

Above all, we should remember this: there is no need ever to be afraid of truth as it is given us in the Word of God. There is no need ever to apologize for anything in Scripture, providing that we understand it rightly. Not even the authority of a great reformer like Luther is sufficient to warrant us to look down upon or neglect any portion of the Bible. "All Scripture is given by inspiration of God, and is profitable for doctrine, for reproof, for correction, for instruction in righteousness: that the man of God may be perfect, thoroughly furnished unto all good works" (II Tim. 3:16, 17). James may not be a doctrinal writer, although his epistle is not devoid of this element; but when it comes to reproof, correction, and instruction in righteousness, he has a major contribution to make. It is certainly true that no Christian can give this little book serious study and apply it in his life without being more "throughly furnished unto all good works" than he was before considering its message.

II

We turn now to the important question of the authorship of the epistle. Who was the James who wrote this remarkable letter? In answering the question we observe that the New Testament speaks of three men called "James." Of these, two were among the twelve disciples (Matt. 10:2, 3). First, there was James, the son of Zebedee and the brother of John. However, his martyrdom by Herod was so early (c. A.D. 44, Acts 12:1, 2) and the church in Jerusalem was then so young that scholars generally rule him out as a possible author of the letter. Secondly, there was James, the son of Alphaeus, sometimes called "James the Less." He, too, was among the Twelve. Yet he is mentioned only a few times in the New Testament and then only in lists of names. Surely it is unlikely that one so obscure would have held the place of authority that the writer of this epistle so clearly had. This leaves us the third New Testament James. In Galatians 1:19 he is called by Paul "James the brother of the Lord," and in Galatians 2:9 Paul speaks of him as a "pillar." Matthew mentions him (13:55) as one of our Saviour's brethren.[1]

This third James was one of the brothers, according to the flesh, of our Lord Jesus Christ. During our Lord's earthly ministry and life, His brothers did not believe on Him (John 7:5). But later James was converted. I Corinthians 15:7 tells us how this happened; the risen Saviour graciously appeared specially and individually to this unbelieving brother. James became the head of the church at Jerusalem. Acts 15 shows him in a position of undoubted leadership there. In

[1] The Scofield Reference Bible (cf. the note on Matthew 4:21) identifies this James with James, the son of Alphaeus, but very few scholars today would agree with this interpretation which involves making "brethren" in Matthew 4:21 mean "cousins," an unnecessary adoption of the Roman Catholic view of our Lord's family.

the early Church he was a man of immense authority. Traditionally called "James the Just," he had a great reputation for holiness. His knees were said to have been calloused through incessant kneeling in prayer. According to tradition, he was martyred, and so great was the esteem in which he was held that his death caused a revolt of the people. Whatever be the factual basis of these stories, they show something of the veneration in which he was held.

It is this James who wrote the epistle we are about to study. Let us bear the fact in mind, for it explains much. Even if we did not know the author, we should have to infer that it must have been someone very close to our Lord. For of all the epistles, that of James is nearer the Sermon on the Mount than any other. It is possible to find in the epistle no less than twenty-two references to the sermon. In some form each of the beatitudes is alluded to. In his style, which is picturesque and powerful, and in his whole manner of thought, James shows what we may call a family resemblance to his divine Brother. From the literary point of view, the epistle is a masterpiece. It is a book stamped as it were with the mind of Christ. Observe, for example, the frequent use of figures drawn from nature, a leading characteristic of our Lord's own manner of speech.

III

We come next to the time of writing. It is not possible to fix the exact year in which the book was written, but we can say with confidence that it was very early and may even have been composed a little before A.D. 50. In all probability it is in point of time the first of the New Testament writings.

There is a certain prestige even today that goes with ecclesiastical priority. The *First* Church of a particular denomination in such-and-such a city has a special share of esteem. Some Christian groups take pride in the long antiquity of their history. Here, in this epistle, we have a book by the head of the very first Christian church—not at Rome, or Corinth, or Ephesus, but at Jerusalem, where Christianity began. Therefore we shall do well to heed its message as, through these studies, it speaks to our hearts.

IV

What about the structure of the epistle? Actually the letter is such that a strictly logical analysis is very difficult. More than that, such analysis is in this case highly questionable. For what James wrote under the inspiration of the Spirit of God is not so much a reasoned argument as a series of sententious sayings clustered round certain recurring themes. In some places he speaks in burning words; always he is in earnest. In manner of expression he is eloquent and beautiful. As someone has said of his book, it is "less a train of thought than a string of pearls."

We therefore shall not attempt any analysis or outline of the epistle. Rather shall we study it as a living document, confronting us with the deep ethical implications of the Gospel and showing us how to "walk worthy of the vocation wherewith we are called." For James is above all a practical book. As John Bunyan put it in *The Pilgrim's Progress:* "The soul of religion is the practical part." Or, as John Wesley said: "The problem of problems is to get Christianity put into practice." As we go on with our study of James, let us, then, be willing to have the inspired words of this letter search our hearts and show us how in our own lives we may more faithfully practice the faith that we hold so dear.

ON READING THE BIBLE

Particularly the Epistle of James

OF ALL BOOKS in the world the Bible is most frequently and at the same time most inadequately read. The chief error in its use is that of piecemeal reading. Even among earnest Christians, there is too much fragmentary perusal of the Word of God and too little thoughtful, consecutive study. Yet the fact remains that the best way to read Scripture, as well as any other book, is to read it as much as possible in its natural units, passing by the chapter divisions, which so often interrupt the flow of thought.

Actually, the Bible is unusually well adapted to such reading. Among its sixty-six books, over thirty are short enough to be finished at one sitting of a half hour or less. As for the larger books, they may be read in logical units that go beyond the usual chapter divisions.

There are, to be sure, many methods of Bible study. But underlying them all is the initial grasp of the separate book or unit as a whole. Nothing is more important for the serious student of Scripture than to learn to read the individual books consecutively with a sensitiveness to their original message. Whoever takes a portion of the Bible, whether it be an epistle like James, a story like Ruth, or a gospel like Mark, and reads it through once, twice, thrice, and even four or five times, with a receptive mind and heart *before* consulting commentaries cannot but be strengthened in the inner man and built up in his faith.

The Epistle of James is a compact little book, so terse in expression that one may sit down and read it through within a period of twenty minutes. With this in mind, it is here printed as an indispensable introduction to the chapters that follow. The reader is not only urged but also challenged to preface his perusal of the commentary with the consecutive reading of James as a unit once daily for at least five days. To do this thoughtfully and prayerfully may well be a memorable experience in the perennial power of the Word of God.

THE EPISTLE OF ST. JAMES

CHAPTER ONE

JAMES, A SERVANT of God and of the Lord Jesus Christ, to the twelve tribes which are scattered abroad, greeting.

My brethren, count it all joy when ye fall into divers temptations; knowing this, that the trying of your faith worketh patience. But let patience have her perfect work, that ye may be perfect and entire, wanting nothing.

If any of you lack wisdom, let him ask of God, that giveth to all men liberally and upbraideth not, and it shall be given him. But let him ask in faith, nothing wavering. For he that wavereth is like a wave of the sea driven with the wind and tossed. For let not that man think that he shall receive any thing of the Lord. A double minded man is unstable in all his ways.

Let the brother of low degree rejoice in that he is exalted, but the rich, in that he is made low: because as the flower of the grass he shall pass away. For the sun is no sooner risen with a burning heat, but it withereth the grass, and the flower thereof falleth, and the grace of the fashion of it perisheth: so also shall the rich man fade away in his ways.

Blessed is the man that endureth temptation: for when he is tried, he shall receive the crown of life, which the Lord hath promised to them that love him. Let no man say when he is tempted, I am tempted of God: for God cannot be tempted with evil, neither tempteth he any man. But every man is tempted, when he is drawn away of his own lust, and enticed. Then when lust hath conceived, it bringeth forth sin: and sin, when it is finished, bringeth forth death. Do not err, my beloved brethren. Every good gift and every perfect gift is from above, and cometh down from the Father of lights, with whom is no variableness, neither shadow of turning. Of his own will begat he us with the word of truth, that we should be a kind of firstfruits of his creatures.

Wherefore, my beloved brethren, let every man be swift to hear, slow to speak, slow to wrath: for the wrath of man worketh not the righteousness of God. Wherefore lay apart all filthiness and superfluity of naughtiness, and receive with meekness the engrafted word, which is able to save your souls. But be ye doers of the word, and not hearers only, deceiving your own selves. For if any be a hearer of the word, and not a doer, he is like unto a man beholding his natural face in a glass: for he beholdeth himself, and goeth his way, and straightway forgetteth what manner of man he was. But whoso looketh into the perfect law of liberty, and continueth therein, he being not a forgetful hearer, but a doer of the work, this man shall be blessed in his deed.

If any man among you seem to be religious, and bridleth not his tongue, but deceiveth his own heart, this man's religion is vain. Pure religion and undefiled before God and the Father is this, to visit the fatherless and widows in their affliction, and to keep himself unspotted from the world.

CHAPTER TWO

MY BRETHREN, HAVE not the faith of our Lord Jesus Christ, the Lord of glory, with respect of persons. For if there come unto your assembly a man with a gold ring, in goodly apparel, and there come in also a poor man in vile raiment, and ye have respect to him that weareth the gay clothing, and say unto him, Sit thou here in a good place; and say to the poor, Stand thou there, or sit here under my footstool: are ye not then partial in yourselves, and are become judges of evil thoughts? Hearken, my beloved brethren, hath not God chosen the poor of this world rich in faith, and heirs of the kingdom which he hath promised to them that love him? But ye have despised the poor. Do not rich men oppress you, and draw you before the judgment seats? Do not they blaspheme that worthy name by the which ye are called?

If ye fulfil the royal law according to the scripture, Thou shalt love thy neighbour as thyself, ye do well: but if ye have respect to persons, ye commit sin, and are convinced of the law as transgressors. For whosoever shall keep the whole law, and yet offend in one point, he is guilty of all. For he that said, Do not commit adultery, said also, Do not kill. Now if thou commit no adultery, yet if thou kill, thou art become a transgressor of the law. So speak ye, and so do, as they that shall be judged by the law of liberty. For he shall have judgment without mercy, that hath shewed no mercy; and mercy rejoiceth against judgment. What doth it profit, my brethren, though a man say he hath faith, and have not works? Can faith save him? If a brother or sister be naked, and destitute of daily food, and one of you say unto them, Depart in peace, be ye warmed and filled; notwithstanding ye give them not those things which are needful to the body; what doth it profit? Even so faith, if it hath not works, is dead, being alone.

Yea, a man may say, Thou hast faith, and I have works: shew me thy faith without thy works, and I will shew thee my faith by my works. Thou believest that there is one God; thou doest well: the devils also believe, and tremble. But wilt thou know, O vain man, that faith without works is dead? Was not Abraham our father justified by works, when he had offered Isaac his son upon the altar? Seest thou how faith wrought with his works, and by works was faith made perfect? And the scripture was fulfilled which saith, Abraham believed God, and it was imputed unto him for righteousness: and he was called the Friend of God. Ye see then how that by works a man is justified, and not by faith only. Likewise also was not Rahab the harlot justified by works, when she had received the messengers, and had sent them out another way? For as the body without the spirit is dead, so faith without works is dead also.

CHAPTER THREE

MY BRETHREN, BE not many masters, knowing that we shall receive the greater condemnation. For in many things we offend all. If any man offend not in word, the same is a perfect man, and able also to bridle the whole body. Behold, we put bits in the horses' mouths, that they may obey us; and we turn about their whole body. Behold also the ships, which though they be so great, and are driven of fierce winds, yet are they turned about with a very small helm, whithersoever the governor listeth. Even so the tongue is a little member, and boasteth great things. Behold, how great a matter a little fire kindleth!

And the tongue is a fire, a world of iniquity: so is the tongue among our members, that it defileth the whole body, and setteth on fire the course of nature, and it is set on fire of hell. For every kind of beasts, and of birds, and of serpents, and of things in the sea, is tamed, and hath been tamed of mankind: but the tongue can no man tame; it is an unruly evil, full of deadly poison. Therewith bless we God, even the Father; and therewith curse we men, which are made after the similitude of God. Out of the same mouth proceedeth blessing and cursing. My brethren, these things ought not so to be. Doth a fountain send forth at the same place sweet water and bitter? Can the fig tree, my brethren, bear olive berries? Either a vine, figs? So can no fountain both yield salt water and fresh.

Who is a wise man and endued with knowledge among you? Let him shew out of a good conversation his works with meekness of wisdom. But if ye have bitter envying and strife in your hearts, glory not, and lie not against the truth. This wisdom descendeth not from above, but is earthly, sensual, devilish. For where envying and strife is, there is confusion and every evil work. But the wisdom that is from above is first pure, then peaceable, gentle, and easy to be intreated, full of mercy and good fruits, without partiality, and without hypocrisy. And the fruit of righteousness is sown in peace of them that make peace.

CHAPTER FOUR

FROM WHENCE COME wars and fightings among you? Come they not hence, even of your lusts that war in your members? Ye lust, and have not: ye kill, and desire to have, and cannot obtain: ye fight and war, yet ye have not, because ye ask not. Ye ask, and receive not, because ye ask amiss, that ye may consume it upon your lusts. Ye adulterers and adulteresses, know ye not that the friendship of the world is enmity with God? Whosoever therefore will be a friend of the world is the enemy of God.

Do ye think that the scripture saith in vain, The spirit that dwelleth in us lusteth to envy? But he giveth more grace. Wherefore he saith, God resisteth the proud, but giveth grace unto the humble. Submit yourselves therefore to God. Resist the devil, and he will flee from you. Draw nigh to God, and he will draw nigh to you. Cleanse your hands, ye sinners; and purify your hearts, ye double minded. Be afflicted, and mourn, and weep: let your laughter be turned to mourning, and your joy to heaviness. Humble yourselves in the sight of the Lord, and he shall lift you up.

Speak not evil one of another, brethren. He that

speaketh evil of his brother, and judgeth his brother, speaketh evil of the law, and judgeth the law: but if thou judge the law, thou art not a doer of the law, but a judge. There is one lawgiver, who is able to save and to destroy: who art thou that judgest another?

Go to now, ye that say, To day or to morrow we will go into such a city, and continue there a year, and buy and sell, and get gain: whereas ye know not what shall be on the morrow. For what is your life? It is even a vapour, that appeareth for a little time, and then vanisheth away. For that ye ought to say, If the Lord will, we shall live, and do this, or that. But now ye rejoice in your boastings: all such rejoicing is evil. Therefore to him that knoweth to do good, and doeth it not, to him it is sin.

CHAPTER FIVE

GO TO NOW, ye rich men, weep and howl for your miseries that shall come upon you. Your riches are corrupted, and your garments are motheaten. Your gold and silver is cankered, and the rust of them shall be a witness against you, and shall eat your flesh as it were fire. Ye have heaped treasure together for the last days. Behold, the hire of the labourers who have reaped down your fields, which is of you kept back by fraud, crieth: and the cries of them which have reaped are entered into the ears of the Lord of sabaoth. Ye have lived in pleasure on the earth, and been wanton; ye have nourished your hearts, as in a day of slaughter. Ye have condemned and killed the just; and he doth not resist you.

Be patient therefore, brethren, unto the coming of the Lord. Behold, the husbandman waiteth for the precious fruit of the earth, and hath long patience for it, until he receive the early and latter rain. Be ye also patient; stablish your hearts: for the coming of the Lord draweth nigh. Grudge not one against another, brethren, lest ye be condemned: behold, the judge standeth before the door.

Take, my brethren, the prophets, who have spoken in the name of the Lord, for an example of suffering affliction, and of patience. Behold, we count them happy which endure. Ye have heard of the patience of Job, and have seen the end of the Lord; that the Lord is very pitiful, and of tender mercy. But above all things, my brethren, swear not, neither by heaven, neither by the earth, neither by any other oath: but let your yea be yea; and your nay, nay, lest ye fall into condemnation.

Is any among you afflicted? Let him pray. Is any merry? Let him sing psalms. Is any sick among you? Let him call for the elders of the church, and let them pray over him, anointing him with oil in the name of the Lord: and the prayer of faith shall save the sick, and the Lord shall raise him up; and if he have committed sins, they shall be forgiven him. Confess your faults one to another, and pray one for another, that ye may be healed. The effectual fervent prayer of a righteous man availeth much. Elias was a man subject to like passions as we are, and he prayed earnestly that it might not rain: and it rained not on the earth by the space of three years and six months. And he prayed again, and the heaven gave rain, and the earth brought forth her fruit.

Brethren, if any of you do err from the truth, and one convert him, let him know that he which converteth the sinner from the error of his way shall save a soul from death, and shall hide a multitude of sins.

THE PRACTICAL EPISTLE OF JAMES

Studies in Applied Christianity

Chapter One

TRIAL AND ENDURANCE

JAMES, A SERVANT *of God and of the Lord Jesus Christ, to the twelve tribes which are scattered abroad, greeting* (1:1). The epistle begins with the formal salutation customary in ancient letters. There is more than casual significance in James's designation of himself. He does not stand upon his authority as head of the church at Jerusalem, but calls himself simply "a servant of God and of the Lord Jesus Christ." The word translated "servant" is the common Greek term, *doulos,* meaning "slave."

There is a lesson in the humility with which James leaves it to others to call him "the brother of the Lord" or a "pillar" of the church. For him the highest honor is to be "a slave of God and of the Lord Jesus Christ." In point of fact, the title is not one to be lightly assumed. It implies a completeness of obedience and depth of consecration very few have any right to claim.

We may be certain that James used it in all humility; yet behind that humility there stands a degree of commitment that makes the title of a "slave" of the Lord the highest Christian designation. Measured by such a standard, how many who say of themselves, "I'm only a servant of the Lord," are really what they claim to be? How many of us are truly *douloi,* "slaves" of the Lord Jesus Christ, obedient to Him in all things, surrendered to His will in every area of our lives?

Consider next the way in which James refers to Christ. The man who, during the earthly life of his divine Brother refused to believe in Him, now gives Him His full title, "the Lord Jesus Christ." Without going so far as to say that it is never permissible to refer to our Saviour in any other way than as "the Lord Jesus Christ," we may see in the title which James gives Him a wholesome corrective to the informal way in which our Lord is so frequently addressed. While we call Him "Jesus," let us not forget that there are many times in our worship and in speaking of Him to others when we should accord Him His full title: the Lord Jesus Christ.

Having identified himself, James now makes clear to whom the epistle is addressed. He is writing, he tells his readers, "to the twelve tribes which are scattered abroad." By this is meant the great company of Jews, known as "the dispersion." In the first century, just as in this twentieth century, the majority of the nation was living not in Palestine but in non-Jewish territory. At the time of Christ, for every Jew in Palestine there were two in dispersion. As the Sybilline Oracle said in the second century of these scattered Jews: "Every land and every sea is full of thee." The initial cause of this dispersion was the Assyrian and Babylonian captivities. Subsequently, Egypt and Syria took numbers of the Jews into bondage. Voluntary emigration also added to the growing multitude of exiles.

It is to the Christian believers among these Jews, "scattered abroad" in the first instance by divine retribution upon the national sin of idolatry, and including in their number representatives of each of the twelve tribes, that James is writing. Let us not make the mistake, however, of thinking that what he has to say is not for us Christians today. As with so much of Scripture, this epistle is addressed first of all to a specific situation. The Word of God has timeless relevancy; the better we understand the particular historical background out of which any portion of it comes, the better are we prepared to grasp the meaning of that portion for us of a later and different age.

As a matter of fact, the first century was strangely like our twentieth century. With all its social and moral corruption, it was a time of expectation of a new and better world. Even such a pre-Christian pagan writer as Virgil spoke in veiled terms of a coming ruler and a golden age. So today, beneath all the turmoil and darkness of our times, men are looking and longing for "a brave, new world" in which there will be peace in place of war and security in place of fear. But what so few understand is the plain fact that the Word of God sets forth the sure hope of the realization of the peace and security for which mankind longs, as it shows us that only through the coming of the Prince of Peace will the world see a better day.

One more fact should be kept in mind regarding "the dispersion." They are still with us. Throughout nineteen hundred years the identity of the Jews has been preserved. Subjected to persecution such as no other people has ever had to endure, they remain the unique race. Like the bush which burned without being consumed, they are indestructible. Nothing—no Russian pogroms of a former generation nor any German Buchenwalds of our time—has been able to destroy them. And today, while Jewish nationalism has been revived in the State of Israel, the dispersion is still world-wide and the twelve tribes are still scattered abroad.

Concluding his salutation, James adds the single word, "greeting." A common expression of courtesy, the word literally means *rejoice*. It is interesting to observe that it occurs at the beginning of the letter sent out by the first Jerusalem Council, headed by James.[1]

[1] Acts 15:23.

Perhaps it was a favorite salutation of the brother of the Lord. But be that as it may, it provides an excellent transition to the first subject which James treats, that of rejoicing in the midst of the trials that inevitably come to every Christian life.

My brethren, count it all joy when ye fall into divers temptations; knowing this, that the trying of your faith worketh patience. But let patience have her perfect work, that ye may be perfect and entire, wanting nothing (1:2-4). It is an amazing statement that we have in verse 2. James is saying nothing less than this: "My brothers, reckon it nothing but joy when you find yourselves in the midst of all sorts of trials and tribulation." Actually most Christians do exactly the opposite; they make trial an occasion for groaning and bewailing their hard circumstances. But James reminds us that testing should be accepted with joy. And why should it not be? For after all, every new trial that comes into our lives is another opportunity for God to show Himself mighty in delivering us. It is all very well to talk about "the victorious life." In actual practice, however, an acid test of victorious living is whether or not trial is really a thing of Christian joy.

Following his statement of the principle of rejoicing in testing, James goes on to explain why Christians should welcome trial. "The trying of your faith," he says, "works patience." "Patience" is the essential quality of endurance, of keeping on in adversity and not giving up; and the "perfect" (the word means *complete*) issue of endurance (vs. 4) is to make us "perfect and entire," or, in other words, "complete and mature." The thought is that of adult Christian character, the result of joyful perseverance amid all manner of testing.

If any of you lack wisdom, let him ask of God, that giveth to all men liberally and upbraideth not, and it shall be given him. But let him ask in faith, nothing wavering. For he that wavereth is like a wave of the sea driven with the wind and tossed. For let not that man think that he shall receive any thing of the Lord. A double minded man is unstable in all his ways (1:5-8). This first chapter of James is like a seed plot. As the writer passes from subject to subject, he touches upon the various themes dealt with in the course of the epistle. Thus, turning at this point from his reference to trial and endurance in the Christian life, a subject to which he is to revert more than once,[2] James introduces the topic of wisdom. He does this by putting before us a promise.

Someone has estimated that there are in the Word of God no less than 3,000 precious promises. Of these, the one recorded in the verses before us is by no means the last. It is, however, one thing to know that Scripture contains such a vast treasure of promises; it is another thing really *to know the promises.* After all, the promises are given not for our admiration but for our use.

[2] Cf. 1:2-15; 4:10-11.

Really to use them we must first of all know them. And then, knowing them, we must put them to the test of experience. This we do by applying them in specific circumstances through believing them.

Now the promise given in James 1:5-8 is one of the most universally applicable in all the Bible. Consider to whom it is addressed: "If any of you lack wisdom . . ." That, of course, includes every human being. We all need wisdom, and we need it over and over again. Life presents a succession of decisions. Time and again we find ourselves searching for the right answer to some perplexity in human relationships, in Christian work, or in our daily business or profession. We realize that the problem is too much for us, and in that very realization, humbling as it is, lies the seed of the solution. For lacking wisdom and acknowledging this lack, we ask God for the wisdom we do not have.

Observe how James, in stating this promise, speaks of God. He is the God that gives to all freely, the God who loves to supply the need of those who come to Him in their ignorance, soliciting the aid of divine omniscience. To such He gives wisdom and, in doing so, He never upbraids them for their ignorance.

The promise, however, has a condition: wisdom must be asked for in faith. When we come to God in our perplexity, frankly acknowledging our ignorance, we must believe that wisdom will be given us. "But what," someone enquires, "is meant by asking in faith?" The answer to that question depends upon the definition of faith. Therefore, we think back to Hebrews 11:1, where we read: "Faith is the substance of things hoped for, the evidence of things not seen." The key to the definition lies in the word "substance," a modern synonym of which is "title-deed" or "guarantee."[3] To have faith, then, is to hope for something to the extent that one believes he has it as surely as if he held in his hand a legal guarantee or title-deed of its accomplishment. Such faith is nothing less than the "evidence," the "conviction," the convinced assurance of that which is not yet actually before one's eyes. Moreover, this attitude must be maintained unwaveringly.

At this point, James illustrates the principle he is pressing home to his readers. In vivid words he compares the vacillating man who says he believes but then doubts, to an ocean wave, driven hither and yon at the mercy of the wind. Here is the first instance in the epistle of a leading trait of James's style—the use of figures drawn from nature. Here, too, we see for the first time his kinship of mind with his divine Brother, whose teaching was full of references to the world of nature.

Having shown so picturesquely that vacillation is incompatible with the steadfast faith that takes God's promises seriously, James completes his characteriza-

[3] The meaning of the Greek word *hypostasis* has, in recent years, been clarified by the Greek papyri.

tion of the waverer with this terse comment: "a double-minded man is unstable in all his ways." The adjective, "double-minded," literally means "two-souled," an apt description of the Christian who is one moment trusting the Lord and another moment doubting Him. Certainly one of the great needs of our times is for whole-hearted, whole-souled Christians. There are all too many in the churches who fit the definition someone gave of half-heartedness as "serving the Lord in such a way as not to offend the devil."

Let the brother of low degree rejoice in that he is exalted, but the rich, in that he is made low: because as the flower of the grass he shall pass away. For the sun is no sooner risen with a burning heat, but it withereth the grass, and the flower thereof falleth, and the grace of the fashion of it perisheth: so also shall the rich man fade away in his ways (1:9-11). The next three verses give us an example of a particular kind of trial and, at the same time, introduce a subject that is later to become one of the major themes of the epistle.[4] The example is a change in the circumstances of life; the theme is the transitoriness of earthly riches. First James mentions the poor with whom he has the deepest sympathy. For "the brother of low degree" to be exalted is obviously a change in status that should lead to rejoicing. But for the rich to lose his wealth and the social privilege that accompanies it is a great trial.

[4] Cf. 2:13; 5:1-6.

Nevertheless, James reminds the rich that such being "made low" should also be a cause of rejoicing. Then, speaking again like his divine Brother, he turns to nature for an illustration, reminding the rich that all things human are transitory. As the grass, the rich will wither away in a short time. Therefore, if the wealthy are humbled, this change in status should be welcomed as an evidence of the common humanity which all men without exception share.

Blessed is the man that endureth temptation: for when he is tried, he shall receive the crown of life, which the Lord hath promised to them that love Him (1:12). As has been already pointed out in these studies, the similarity of outlook between James and the Lord Jesus is marked. A rewarding study, for instance, is to compare the epistle with the Sermon on the Mount. Such comparison reveals many parallels.

For example, James now gives us a beatitude upon the subject of trial or testing.[5] The blessing, he points out, is for the man who "endures" temptation; it is for the man who has the patience spoken of in verses 3 and 4 of this chapter. Such a man will, when he has stood the test, receive a reward, called here "the crown of life." But this reward is promised, not indiscriminately but only to them that love the Lord. The beati-

[5] The word "temptation" should here be interpreted in this broader sense of *testing;* it includes, of course, temptation in the sense of solicitation to evil, but goes beyond that to comprehend trials in general.

tude, therefore, is combined with a promise. It is not just endurance under trial, holding out against temptation, that is singled out for blessedness and reward. After all, there is a sort of stoical patience that keeps on through the most severe testing and yet, admirable as it may be, is far from Christian. The endurance of the Christian is of quite another order; its difference is in respect to love. The crown of life will be given only to those who, enduring trial and standing the test, *love* the Lord; it is promised only "to them that love Him." Thus James very early in his epistle stresses the great differential which sets Christian virtue apart from any other standard of conduct.

Chapter Two

TEMPTATION AND REALITY

LET NO MAN *say when he is tempted, I am tempted of God: for God cannot be tempted with evil, neither tempteth He any man. But every man is tempted when he is drawn away of his own lust, and enticed. Then when lust hath conceived, it bringeth forth sin: and sin, when it is finished, bringeth forth death* (1:13-15). It is important for the understanding of Scripture, or, for that matter, any other book, to bear in mind the principle that the meaning of a word is often affected by its context. An illustration of this principle is found in the usage of "temptation" in this first chapter of James. In its broad meaning, the word[1] translated "temptation" signifies "trial" or "testing."[2] But it also

[1] Greek *peirasmos*.

[2] Cf., for example, Acts 5:9, where Peter accuses Sapphira of "tempting" (Grk. *peiradzō*) the Spirit of the Lord. Here the meaning is obviously "testing," for the Spirit of God could not be tempted to do evil.

has the more familiar sense of *solicitation to do evil.* As we have already seen, in verse 2 the word has the broader significance of "testing." In the passage before us, however, it clearly relates to the more restricted idea of "incitement to evil or sin." The pivot on which the thought swings over to the more specific usage seems to be in verse 12, in which the beatitude of the man who endures temptation is declared and the reward of the crown of life is promised him. The temptation so endured is thought of, then, in the broad sense of a test, but the test obviously includes actual solicitation to evil, along with trial and adversity, as verses 13-15 clearly imply.

James begins this passage, which is a wonderful analysis of temptation in the evil sense, with a warning. Whenever, he is saying, anyone of us is tempted to sin, let him beware of blaming the temptation on God. To do this is a contradiction in terms, because God, being perfectly holy, is Himself "untemptable," or, as James puts it, He "*cannot* be tempted with evil." Therefore, in the sense of soliciting to evil, He never tempts any man.

But if our temptations to sin cannot originate with God, whence do they come? James is not slow to answer the question. Just as Darwin wrote on *The Origin of the Species,* James now discusses the origin of temptation; but, whereas Darwin dealt with his subject in hundreds of thousands of words, James compresses his profound inquiry into less than forty words.

Where does temptation come from? James quickly replies that it comes from within ourselves; we are solicited to sin by the lust that resides in our human nature. This, of course, is exactly in accord with the teaching of James's divine Brother. Defilement, the Lord Jesus pointed out, comes not "from without a man . . . but the things which come out of him, those are they that defile a man." And He went on to list the tragic progeny of the unregenerate heart: "For from within, out of the heart of men, proceed evil thoughts, adulteries, fornications, murders, thefts, covetousness, wickedness, deceit, lasciviousness, an evil eye, blasphemy, pride, foolishness: all these evil things come from within, and defile the man."[3]

The next verse is phrased in biological language, giving us in effect the genesis of sin. It is lust, our own evil desire, that conceives, the result of this conception being sin. But conception and birth require a father. And though James does not, in this condensed but searching analysis of temptation, mention the father, it can be no other than the devil himself. The child, then, who is conceived in the matrix of our own lust through the agency of Satan is sin. "And sin," James continues, "when it is finished, bringeth forth death." How true that is! The whole record of history bears

[3] Mark 7:15, 21-23.

witness to the fact that, as Ezekiel declares, "The soul that sinneth it shall die,"[4] and, as Paul affirms, "The wages of sin is death."[5]

Do not err, my beloved brethren. Every good gift and every perfect gift is from above, and cometh down from the Father of lights, with whom is no variableness, neither shadow of turning (1:16, 17). The exhortation of verse 16 is needed in our age of confused moral and spiritual values. Using his favorite form of address to his readers ("my brethren") James urges them not to "err." The meaning of the Greek word thus translated is considerably stronger than our English "err"; it is a verb that was used of a ship driven from its course. Thus it reminds us of the necessity of not being driven through temptation and sin from the way of life in Christ.

But if temptation can issue in sin, conceived through our human lust, this is only one aspect of life. There is also, in contrast to the dark progeny of temptation, an abundance of good gifts. These James proceeds to trace directly to God. Their origin is heavenly ("from above"); they come down from "the Father of lights," a unique appellation of God, reminding us of the majestic word recorded in Genesis 1: "And God said, Let there be light: and there was light."[6] There follows a

[4] Ezekiel 18:4.
[5] Romans 6:23.
[6] Genesis 1:3.

clause in which "the Father of lights" is defined as being without "variableness, neither shadow of turning." Here the word translated "variableness" is the term from which our English "parallax" comes. A definition of this rather uncommon word will help us understand what James is saying. According to the dictionary, "parallax" means "the apparent change in position of an object, due to change in position of the observer." The thought is plainly that of God's immutability. What a comforting reminder this is in an unstable world! Our God is not only the source of "every good and every perfect gift"; He is also absolutely unchangeable. Whatever there seems to be of variation in Him is only apparent, for like the parallax it is the result of a shift in our position, not in Him. It is this central truth about God that the author of the Epistle to the Hebrews expresses in Christocentric form in the memorable declaration: "Jesus Christ the same yesterday, and today, and forever."[7]

Of His own will begat He us with the Word of truth, that we should be a kind of firstfruits of His creatures (1:18). One of the catch-phrases used by some commentators on James is that his epistle contains "no Gospel." While it is true that, from the doctrinal point of view, he does not touch upon many of the doctrines developed in Paul's epistles, it is less than fair to label James's teaching as "elementary" and of secondary

[7] Hebrews 13:8.

value. We might just as well call much of Christ's teaching "elementary," on the ground that it does not exhibit the full doctrinal development of the Pauline epistles.

Moreover, the charge that James contains "no Gospel" is simply untrue. Consider, for example, this eighteenth verse of the first chapter. Speaking of the unchanging "Father of lights," James tells us that "of His own will" the Father "begat us with the Word of truth." There could hardly be a clearer reference to the new birth than this. It assigns the initiative for regeneration to the Father's own will, it refers to birth ("begat"), and it points to the seed whereby we are reborn—"by the Word of truth." Notice also the similarity between James's statement of regeneration and that of Peter in the latter's First Epistle: "Being born again, not of corruptible seed but of incorruptible, by the Word of God, which liveth and abideth for ever."[8] But even more, James gives us the result of regeneration "with the Word of truth"; it is, he says, "that we should be a kind of firstfruits of His creatures," i. e., of the new order of those begotten by God through His Word.

Wherefore, my beloved brethren, let every man be swift to hear, slow to speak, slow to wrath: for the wrath of man worketh not the righteousness of God. Wherefore lay apart all filthiness and superfluity of naughtiness, and receive with meekness the engrafted Word,

[8] I Peter 1:23.

which is able to save your souls (1:19-21). With the practicality that makes his epistle so valuable to the everyday Christian, James immediately turns to application. He prefaces his appeal to his readers as "my brethren" by the affectionate "beloved," urging them to be alert of comprehension ("swift to hear"), reticent in speech ("slow to speak"), and not easily provoked to anger ("slow to wrath"). Here ("slow to speak") is James's first reference to a subject which was close to his heart and of which in the third chapter, he gives the fullest treatment in all the Bible. His emphasis in this place calls to mind the pastor who had on his desk a motto reading: "Better remain silent and be thought a fool than speak and remove all doubt."

The next phrase, "slow to wrath," introduces a profound statement about anger. Mere human anger, James tells us, is not in itself the agent that brings about the righteousness of God, the implication being that in the nature of the case our human wrath is not to be used as a means for doing good. This thought leads in turn to a call to eschew evil: "lay apart all filthiness and superfluity of naughtiness." Here the King James Version is picturesque but almost unintelligible to the average reader today. Actually, "superfluity of naughtiness" is a strong phrase, suggesting something like this: "the overflowing of wickedness." More important, however, than literary consideration is the meaning of the simple word "all." The challenge is for us to do nothing less than put away from our lives *all* defilement and *all* wickedness. God is never satisfied with partial purity, partial goodness, partial righteousness. While the believer is not in this life experimentally perfect, he can have no higher goal than total goodness, knowing that, as God sees him *in* Christ, he is even now judicially righteous.

But as we put away *all* evil, we are to go on to "receive with meekness the engrafted Word which is able to save our souls." Here is another reference to the Gospel. In plain language James is telling us that salvation is not gained by what we do. So we are to "receive with meekness [humbly] the implanted [engrafted] Word," for it is the medium whereby salvation is communicated to our souls. The bearing of this statement upon the controversy regarding faith and works, occasioned by the latter part of chapter 2, is important. Inspired writers do not contradict themselves. And James, who here attributes salvation to "the implanted Word," will not be found, as we study his second chapter, to attribute this same salvation to human works.

But be ye doers of the Word, and not hearers only, deceiving your own selves. For if any be a hearer of the Word, and not a doer, he is like unto a man beholding his natural face in a glass: for he beholdeth himself, and goeth his way, and straightway forgetteth what manner of man he was. But whoso looketh into the perfect law of liberty, and continueth therein, he being not a forgetful hearer, but a doer of the work, this man shall be blessed in his deed (1:22-25). This paragraph begins with a great principle, tersely stated. For many years New York University used for its chief undergraduate colleges a significant terminology. The division of liberal arts was called "The College of Arts and Pure Science"; the school of engineering was known as "The College of Applied Science." The terminology is suggestive in relation to the emphasis so characteristic of James, who may well be called "The Apostle of Applied Christianity." And never has the challenge of the practical application of the faith been more effectively stated than in this twenty-second verse: "But be ye doers of the Word and not hearers only, deceiving your own selves." There is, however, an important difference between James's practicality and the university terminology to which we have just alluded. The latter implies a gap between theory and practice and designates the liberal arts and sciences as "pure" in distinction to their application. This, of course, is questionable and, from the Christian point of view, quite wrong. For the Bible countenances no such gap between doctrine and practice. Rather is the emphasis upon doing the truth, as John puts it.[9]

Having stated the principle, James illustrates it. The mere hearer of God's Word, he says, who does not practise the truth that he hears is like a man looking in

[9] John 3:21.

a mirror who, having seen his face, walks off, promptly forgetting what the mirror showed him. The picture is a simple one, yet there is a great deal behind it. There is, for example, the phrase translated, "his natural face." Literally, it is "the face of his birth,"[10] the implication of which may well be that, when a man looks into the Word of God, which James calls in the next verse "the perfect law of liberty," he sees himself as he is by nature; i.e., he sees himself as what Paul calls "the natural man."

Continuing our consideration of this illustration of the mirror, we ask ourselves why it is that a man looks into a glass. The answer, many a man might say with a smile, would be different for a woman, because women are commonly thought of as admiring themselves in their mirrors. But a man is more practical; he glances in the looking glass, not for self-admiration but to see whether his face needs shaving or his hair needs trimming. And then, if he goes away without acting upon what he sees, he is foolish indeed.

The application is obvious. To look into the mirror of the Word of God involves an obligation. Bible reading is one of the most important things any Christian can possibly do. But it has its dangers. For anyone to look into the pages of Scripture, to behold "the face of his birth," to see himself as he is, and then to shrug his shoulders and walk away unconcerned about doing

[10] Greek, *To prosōpon tēs geneseōs.*

anything to amend his life—this is perilous. Such use of the Bible can harden one's heart and deaden one's soul. Christian truth, "the perfect law of liberty," is always in order to practise.

The next verse gives the contrasting picture. Here is the man who looks into the divine glass, "the perfect law of liberty," and does something about it. The first thing he does is that he "continueth therein"; he takes not a cursory glance but a long, thoughtful look; he abides in the truth and dwells in it, as it were. Then, remembering what he sees, he goes out to be "a doer of the work," and in the very doing he is blessed.

Before we leave this passage, something should be said of James's characterization of the Word of God as "the perfect law of liberty." The phrase is paradoxical: "law" implies *restraint,* which is something different from the common idea of *liberty.* There is, however, no real conflict. In the Christian sense, there is no liberty outside of submission to the perfect law of God. It is the truth as it is in Christ that makes men free.[11] Submission to the divine law is in its ultimate sense submission to Him who is its whole fulfilment, and in His service there is "perfect freedom."

If any man among you seem to be religious, and bridleth not his tongue, but deceiveth his own heart, this man's religion is vain. Pure religion and undefiled before God and the Father is this, to visit the father-

[11] John 8:32.

less and widows in their affliction, and to keep himself unspotted from the world (1:26, 27). The chapter closes with an immensely important reference to religion and its true nature. To many of us it comes as somewhat of a shock to realize that the word translated "religion"[12] appears only four times in the New Testament. Two of these four times it is used by James in this passage.

What, then, does "religion" in New Testament usage mean? First of all, it is not synonymous with salvation. Nor is it the same thing as Christianity. The word means "outward worship" and relates to the expression of the faith that is in the heart. This being so, we see in the next place that "religion" though not in itself salvation, is vitally necessary. James is constantly concerned with the problem of reality in Christian life and service. So, summing up this opening chapter, he gives an actual picture of what it means to be "a doer of the Word."

It means, he says, these three things: controlling one's speech (bridling the tongue), doing deeds of charity ("to visit the fatherless and widows in their affliction"), and living a pure and separated life ("to keep himself unspotted from the world"). This first is plain enough; again in this opening chapter James stresses the absolute necessity for the Christian to discipline his speech. The second is likewise plain. But let

[12] Greek, *thrēskeia.*

us not be deceived; clarity does not imply triviality or unimportance. It may seem obvious to be reminded of the necessity for a controlled tongue and for serving the Lord through ministering to the unfortunate. But you and I, Christians though we are, cannot be truly religious if we consistently fail in these respects. We may know a great deal about the Bible, we may be expert in the interpretation of prophecy, we may be thoroughly versed in doctrine, but if we have unbridled tongues and if we fail to do works of charity, we are not "religious" in the plain New Testament meaning of that great but misunderstood word. And then, in the third place, James tells us that "pure religion and undefiled" has a qualitative as well as practical aspect. It involves an attitude and purpose—that of keeping oneself "unspotted from the world."

At this point, an anecdote will provide the best exposition. Early in his ministry Dr. Maltbie Babcock, who was the distinguished pastor of the Brick Presbyterian Church in New York, was approached by a physician who was a member of his congregation. The physician, a good friend of Dr. Babcock, was concerned about the health of his pastor, who had been working very hard and clearly needed relaxation. Handing Dr. Babcock some theatre tickets, he said: "Take these, you need the recreation of going to this play."

His pastor looked at them, and seeing that they were

tickets to a play of a kind he could not conscientiously attend, said kindly: "Thank you, but I can't take them. I can't go."

"Why not?" the physician asked. "You're tired and need the entertainment."

Then Dr. Babcock replied somewhat in this way: "Yes, I am tired, and I do need recreation. But, doctor, it's this way. You are a physician, a surgeon, in fact. When you operate you scrub your hands meticulously until you are aseptically clean. You wouldn't dare operate with dirty hands. Well, I am a servant of Christ; I deal with precious human souls. And I wouldn't dare do my work with a dirty life."

The lesson is plain. It applies to every Christian, not just to ministers. Religion in its high, New Testament sense, requires not only sound speech and charitable deeds; it demands also a life that is clean and pure, "unspotted from the world," that Christ-rejecting system surrounding us.

Chapter Three

THE SIN OF PARTIALITY

WHILE THE FIRST chapter of James contains a variety of themes, being, as we have seen, the seed plot of the entire epistle, the second chapter is devoted to a consideration of two chief subjects. In the first thirteen verses, the writer concerns himself with Christian democracy. After laying down the principle (vs. 1) that the faith must not be compromised through a snobbish respect for wealth and position, he draws a picture from the life of the church at Jerusalem (vss. 2-4). Then he applies the lesson to his readers (vss. 5-7) and concludes by revealing the true nature of un-Christian respect of persons (vss. 9-13). The second half of the chapter (vss. 14-26) James devotes to an exposition of the relation of faith to works. In doing this, he writes a passage that has been misunderstood and debated, not through the fault of James but because of the failure of his interpreters to relate it to the whole pattern of the epistle's thought and purpose.

My brethren, have not the faith of our Lord Jesus Christ, the Lord of glory, with respect of persons. For if there come unto your assembly a man with a gold ring, in goodly apparel, and there come in also a poor man in vile raiment, and ye have respect to him that weareth the gay clothing, and say unto him, Sit thou here in a good place; and say to the poor, Stand thou there, or sit here under my footstool: are ye not then partial in yourselves, and are become judges of evil thoughts? (2:1-4). James begins his discussion of true Christian brotherhood by declaring that "respect of persons," by which he means unwarranted deference to people of wealth and position, is incompatible with "the faith of our Lord Jesus Christ, the Lord of glory."

Observe that James now gives his divine brother His complete and rightful title. No longer does he have any question of the full Lordship of Him he had known in the bosom of the family but rejected in days past.

In vivid words James shows us how, even in the very first Christian assemblies, brotherly love had given way to snobbish deference to the rich and unfeeling contempt for the poor. His picture of the lavishly dressed man, fingers resplendent with many gold rings (a badge of wealth in those days) in contrast with the poor man in ragged clothing; his portrayal of eagerness to give the place of honor to ostentatious wealth while relegating the poor to some corner or to the floor—these are drawn from life. James had actually seen such things enacted, and his indignation had been stirred.

Have we not seen the same thing in our churches today? The human heart does not change; we of this twentieth century have also held the faith of our Lord Jesus Christ, the Lord of glory, in respect of persons. Thinking of the rich as potential sources of money for our work, we have sometimes lavished upon them undeserved attention and flattery, while treating the poor with scant courtesy. The plain fact is that such actions, whenever found in the Christian church, reveal deplorable lack of faith. Were we looking wholly to God for help, we should not be making these distinctions. It must also be admitted that few things in the New Testament are more disregarded in Christian work than this principle of not respecting persons. We can only accept the rebuke, saying with new determination to trust God more completely: "Brethren, these things ought not so to be."

With verse five the apostle points the lesson straight at his readers. "Hearken, my beloved brethren," he says, and proceeds to show that God has chosen the poor for special blessings; their poverty leads to riches in faith, for they are heirs of the kingdom. Yet those who despise the poor presume to reverse God's estimate. It was F. B. Meyer, the saintly British expositor, who pointed out that there is nothing men dread more than poverty. They will break every commandment of the Decalogue rather than be poor. But poverty was our Lord's chosen lot. He had one opportunity only of living in this world, and He chose to be born in a home so poor that His family could present for Him in the temple merely two doves.

Not only is contempt for the poor a reversal of God's estimate of men; it is also, James continues, unreasonable in view of the actions of the rich. For it is the rich who, because of their oppression of the common man and their blasphemy of the name of the Lord, really deserve contempt (vss. 6, 7). How foolish, therefore, to defer to the rich, when they are so often unworthy of respect! At heart they, too, are sinners, just as much, if not more, in need of God's grace as are any other human beings.

A story told of Prebendary Wilson Carlisle, founder of the Church Army that ministered to the down-and-out men of London, illustrates this essential quality of all of us. Carlisle was honored by the friendship of King Edward VII, and paid a visit to the king during his last illness. As he stood by the royal bedside, the king said: "Well, Carlisle, what are you telling your men now?" And, before there was time to reply, he continued, "Tell them, Carlisle, that kings and tramps need the same Saviour."

Having revealed the unworthiness of many of the rich, James unmasks the true nature of snobbishness.

It is, he shows (vss. 9-13), nothing less than downright sin. It is sin because it breaks "the royal law" of loving one's neighbor as oneself. Fully as much as flagrant law-breaking like murder or adultery, snobbery makes a person a transgressor. Far from being, as so many think it, a half-permissible social lapse, a small thing in a different category from the "bigger" sins, it is an offense against the very heart of Christianity, which is love. Therefore, to indulge it convicts the snob of violation of the holy law of God.

James's dissection of the sin of snobbery is the classic treatment of this subject in the Bible. He closes it with a stern warning (vss. 12, 13). We are, he says, to speak and act as those who are about to be judged by "the law of liberty." The phrase looks back to the twenty-fifth verse of the first chapter and is synonymous with "the royal law." He who has been unmerciful—and the snob is indeed without mercy—will be judged without mercy; he who has treated his neighbor according to the royal law, the law of liberty, will find that mercy for him will triumph over judgment.

Chapter Four

FAITH AND WORKS

WHAT DOTH IT *profit, my brethren, though a man say he hath faith and have not works? Can faith save him? If a brother or sister be naked, and destitute of daily food, and one of you say unto them, Depart in peace, be ye warmed and filled; notwithstanding ye give them not those things which are needful to the body; what doth it profit? Even so faith, if it hath not works, is dead, being alone. Yea, a man may say, Thou hast faith, and I have works; shew me thy faith without thy works, and I will shew thee my faith by my works. Thou believest that there is one God; thou doest well: the devils also believe, and tremble. But wilt thou know, O vain man, that faith without works is dead? Was not Abraham our father justified by works, when he had offered Isaac his son upon the altar? Seest thou how faith wrought with his works, and by works was faith made perfect? And the Scripture was fulfilled which saith,*

Abraham believed God, and it was imputed unto him for righteousness: and he was called the Friend of God. Ye see then how that by works a man is justified, and not by faith only. Likewise also was not Rahab the harlot justified by works, when she had received the messengers, and had sent them out another way? For as the body without the spirit is dead, so faith without works is dead also (2:14-26).

We are now face to face with the passage that so many, the great Luther included, have misunderstood. Every student of the New Testament knows that Paul teaches the justification of the sinner before a holy God by faith and not by works. In Romans, Galatians, Ephesians, all through his epistles, the apostle to the Gentiles drives home this central truth of Christian theology. But here is James seemingly teaching the very opposite. For does he not say, "Faith, if it hath not works, is dead" (vs. 17), and does he not conclude this second chapter by declaring that "faith without works is dead" (vs. 26)?

What, then, are we to say about this apparent conflict? In the first place, let us see it for what it is—not a species of theological puzzle but a living tissue very close to the heart of personal Christianity. Like everything with which James deals, it is related to practical life. In the next place, let us view it as a representative example of other Bible difficulties. Looking at it in this way, we may learn something of what to do with the hard places in the Scriptures, and there are not a few such places.

How then are Bible difficulties to be dealt with? Always first of all by facing the problem prayerfully in the light of all the Scripture evidence. The facts must be brought into the open and none suppressed. There may be an answer, as in this case of the supposed conflict between James and Paul. Or there may not seem to be any satisfactory answer.

In the latter case, what are we to do? An anecdote will show the Christian attitude in the face of difficulties beyond our present power to explain. The story is about an Episcopal clergyman who took a seat in a dining car on a train traveling along the Hudson River. It happened that opposite him was an atheist. Seeing the clerical collar of his companion, he set out to argue with him and began thus: "I see, sir, that you are a clergyman."

"Yes," was the reply, "I am a minister of the Gospel."

There was a pause, after which the atheist said: "I suppose, then, that you believe the Bible."

Now the clergyman was a man of sound, scriptural faith, so that he replied: "I do indeed believe the Bible to be the Word of God."

Immediately there came the query: "But don't you find things in the Bible you can't understand?"

The minister answered humbly: "Yes, there are places in the Scripture too hard for me to understand."

Whereupon the atheist retorted with an air of triumph, thinking he had his companion cornered: "Well, what do you do then?"

Quietly the minister went on eating his luncheon, which happened to be Hudson River shad, a delicious fish, but noted for the over-development of its bony structure. Then he looked up and said: "I do, sir, just as I do when eating this shad. When I come to the bones, I put them to the side of the plate and go on enjoying my lunch, leaving the bones for some fool to choke on."

The moral of the story is plain. Of course there are hard places in the Bible—problems not yet solved, discrepancies unreconciled, difficulties not fully explained. The wise thing is sometimes to lay them aside, as one goes on with the study of the great truths of Scripture that nourish the soul. Such a procedure is not evasion, provided that the difficulties have been honestly considered. It is rather the exercise of a suspended judgment. And it may well result in problems being solved later on, as they are attacked anew in the light of fresh evidence.

But we must come to grips with the problem before us. Are James and Paul in irreconcilable conflict? That is the question. Four considerations will show that the two are not locked in opposition, as so many have thought.

1. James is not answering Paul. The epistle is too

early (c. A.D. 45) for this to be the case; at that time none of Paul's letters had yet been written. Nor can it be said that Paul in Galatians and Romans, where he so plainly affirms justification by faith, is answering James. While chronology does not forbid this, it is psychologically unlikely. We know quite enough of Paul to realize that, had he felt James to be wrong in his teaching about justification, he would have said so. The apostle, who did not hesitate to withstand Peter "to his face, because he was to be blamed" for his compromising attitude toward the Judaizing party,[1] would not have kept silent regarding James's teaching were it really incompatible with the great principle of faith. But rather than opposing James, Paul evidently held him in high respect.

2. The apparent contradiction is not accidental. The Bible is the inspired Word of God, and there are no accidents with Him who inspired it. Consequently, we must conclude that this passage is in the New Testament for a purpose. And that purpose can only be to fix our attention upon an important but neglected truth.

3. The so-called contradiction is merely formal—in words but not in underlying truth. At bottom, there is no clash in the Pauline and Jamesian views of justification. Rather do they complement one another, fitting together to give the complete view of the subject.

[1] Galatians 2:9-21.

4. This being the case, the key to the problem is twofold. It depends, first, upon the principle of language that the same word may in differing contexts have varying meanings, and, secondly, upon the fact that Paul and James look upon justification from quite different points of view.

Let us consider for a moment the principle that the same word has various meanings. There is, for example, the word "church." In one context, it means "a group of believers" gathered together for worship and service; in another case, it means "an edifice" set apart for worship. Or, take the word "temptation," so prominent in this Epistle of James. Sometimes it means "solicitation to evil," while in another setting it implies "testing" or "trial." But illustrations could be multiplied indefinitely. The plain fact is that the significance of words depends in good part upon their context.

With this in mind, we turn to the key words in the passage before us—"faith," "works," and "justify." As he discusses its relation to works, James uses faith in the sense of mere intellectual orthodoxy, the assent of the head but not the committal of the whole being. This is clear from verse 19: "Thou believest that there is one God; thou doest well: the devils also believe, and tremble." But for Paul, faith, as his epistles abundantly show, means "trust in the redemptive work of the Lord Jesus Christ;" in his thought, it relates to the developed doctrines of grace and implies full committal to the Saviour.

When we come to "works," we find a similar diversity of usage. With James works mean "the works of the believer;" they are the outward evidence of a saved life, the fruit that proves that the individual partakes of the root. On the other hand, Paul, writing somewhat later, gives us a more highly developed doctrine of works. In his epistles he uses the Greek *erga* (works) "dead works," i.e., "deeds of the unregenerate man," whereby man vainly hopes to acquire a meritorious standing before God. He uses the same *erga* for "good works," by which he means "fruit that the justified man must bring forth." In the former case, he generally uses *erga* without an adjective; in the latter case, corresponding to James's "works," he usually adds "good," making his term "good works."

Finally, we look at the verb "justify." Here we examine first Paul's usage, because of its depth and comprehensiveness. In his thought it is a legal, positional term. As the Westminster Shorter Catechism puts it: "Justification is an act of God's free grace, wherein He pardoneth all our sins, and accepteth us as righteous in His sight, only for the righteousness of Christ imputed to us, and received by faith alone." It relates to the initial moment of the Christian life, and is a once-and-for-all act. In contrast is James's concept of justification; for him it pertains to any after moment of the

Christian life and describes the vindication of a man before his fellow-men, not before God. Or, to put it in another way, in their views of justification Paul and James complement one another. Paul deals with the root of initial acceptance with God which is wholly by grace through faith; James is concerned with the subsequent and continuing proof of the reality of the initial transaction. It was the great expositor Bengel who said that upon the definition of twenty words the understanding of the whole of Scripture depends. Surely among these twenty words the three we have been considering—"works," "faith," and "justify"—must be numbered.

We now turn to specific comment on verses 14-26. The tone of the passage is set in verse fourteen. Observe that James begins by asking what profit there is if a man "say" (the word with its connotation of externality is significant) he has faith and has not works. "Can that faith [in the original the definite article precedes 'faith'] save him?" Clearly it is a mere verbal faith that the Lord's brother has in mind.

The next two verses (15, 16) illustrate the futility of empty words when deeds of charity are demanded. It is worthy of note that John uses a similar illustration in his First Epistle (3:17, 18), but that he does so in relation to love rather than faith. In the following verse James drives home the illustration: "Even so faith by itself, if it has not works, is dead" (vs. 17). Again the emphasis is upon the externality of the kind of faith that says much but does nothing.

A vivid little conversation (vs. 18) follows, in which the man who claims to have faith is challenged by one who possesses the works that support faith, after which (vs. 19) James refers to belief in one God as being held also by the demons. Obviously he does not have in mind saving faith but simply intellectual orthodoxy. So he draws the conclusion that faith of the kind just described is "dead"[2] apart from works (vs. 20).

In the succeeding five verses James points to two well-known Old Testament characters, both of whom are used elsewhere in the New Testament as outstanding examples of faith. The first and most important of these two is Abraham, and upon him James places chief emphasis. Here for the first time in the epistle the word "justified" is used. It is Abraham's supreme act of faith in offering Isaac upon the altar that James cites as the "works" whereby Abraham was justified. But in Hebrews 11:17 this same act on the part of Abraham is given as the culminating evidence of his faith. And indeed James recognizes (vs. 22) the indissoluble union of faith and works in this instance, his point being that it was by works (action) that Abraham's faith was perfected (completed, or fulfilled).

All this is, of course, not incompatible with the

[2] The word for "dead" in this sentence means "barren," as of a field that fails to produce, not dead in the physical sense.

Pauline doctrine of justification by faith alone, provided that we keep in mind the fact that throughout this discussion James is thinking of works as the outward evidence of faith. And surely it is no accident that James goes on to quote the same verse (Genesis 15:6) which Paul cites in Romans 4 in proving justification by faith from the life of Abraham.

Much the same can be said of the reference to Rahab (vs. 25). Like Abraham she, too, appears in Hebrews 11, the classic faith chapter, and with her also it is the deed of faith that gives external evidence for others to see the belief she held.

With a striking figure of speech, James concludes the passage. Just as the body without the living spirit is a corpse, so, he says, faith without works is also dead (vs. 26). He has stated the principle with startling force, much as his divine Brother spoke at times in powerful hyperbole. But his emphasis is wholesome and greatly needed by many in evangelical circles today. The idea is paradoxical; by a strange reversal, faith, which is something essentially intangible, is compared to a physical body, while works, which have to do with material things, are compared with the spirit. And there is a sense in which faith *is* a body, as in a system of doctrine or "body" of truth. When so regularized and systematized it comes alive, James reminds us, only by being put into practice, acted upon, or done.

Finally, let us remember that James does not set

forth the final New Testament conclusion on the relation of faith and works. His teaching is a greatly needed corrective to the unreal, verbalistic kind of religion that claims allegiance to high doctrine but issues in living on a low and selfish level. Yet for the full synthesis we must turn to the Epistle to the Ephesians. Here Paul resolves once and for all any seeming contradiction between faith and works. We can do no better, therefore, than to conclude this discussion by quoting his words: "For by grace are ye saved through faith; and that not of yourselves; it is the gift of God: not of works, lest any man should boast. For we are His workmanship, created in Christ Jesus unto good works, which God hath before ordained that we should walk in them" (Eph. 2:8-10). Nothing could be stronger than Paul's repudiation of any other way of salvation than by grace through faith, wholly apart from works; nor could anything be more irresistibly logical than his insistence than the foreordained purpose of our creation as Christians is that we who believe *must* produce good works, the latter being the very truth stressed by James.

Chapter Five

TONGUE CONTROL

MY BRETHREN, BE *not many masters, knowing that we shall receive the greater condemnation. For in many things we offend all. If any man offend not in word, the same is a perfect man, and able also to bridle the whole body* (3:1, 2). Having concluded his analysis of the relation of faith and works, James turns to the one member of the human body most difficult of control. In vivid words he pictures the evil potentiality of the tongue. There is impressive logic in the location of this passage in the center of the epistle, immediately following the great discussion at the close of chapter 2. The writer is saying to the believer something like this: "You claim to have saving faith. Very well, my friend. But what about your tongue? Is it being controlled in faith by the Lord?"

The Bible never makes mistakes in emphasis, and this epistle is no exception to the rule. In Scripture idle words, profane speech, malicious and lying communications, are not regarded lightly. Therefore, James is in the mainstream of biblical ethics as he gives us this classic treatment of the tongue.

The chapter begins with a warning that, in the Authorized Version, is quite unintelligible to the modern reader. The difficulty is with the word "masters," which simply means *teachers.* The writer is first of all reminding his readers that they should not be overanxious to take up the ministry of teaching, because those who teach, being in a place of special responsibility, are especially accountable to God.

In the wider sense, most of us are at one time or another engaged in teaching. Parents, whether they realize it or not, are teachers, and the home cannot escape being a place of instruction. Moreover, teaching goes on constantly in everyday living, in business or profession. Wherever it is done, it carries with it responsibility for the control of our words to God's glory.

After an acknowledgment that we are all transgressors, James uses a startling proposition to show the crucial importance of the tongue (vs. 2). The man who does not offend in word, he says, is a perfect man; managing his tongue, he is able to manage his whole body.

Worthy of comment is the original word for "man." It is not the generic term *anthrōpos,* meaning mankind in general, but *anēr,* designating "man" in distinction from "woman" and meaning also "husband." Apparently James does not share the common male belief that women are chief offenders in the misuse of the tongue. While it would be poor exegesis to press his use of *anēr* to the point of absolving women from wrong use of the tongue, for they are certainly included, yet a moment's reflection shows that men, in their proneness to profanity, blasphemy, and impurity of speech, may well be the greater offenders.

Behold, we put bits in the horses' mouths, that they may obey us; and we turn about their whole body. Behold also the ships, which though they be so great, and are driven of fierce winds, yet are they turned about with a very small helm, whithersoever the governor listeth. Even so the tongue is a little member, and boasteth great things. Behold, how great a matter a little fire kindleth! And the tongue is a fire, a world of iniquity: so is the tongue among our members, that it defileth the whole body, and setteth on fire the course of nature, and it is set on fire of hell. For every kind of beasts, and of birds, and of serpents, and of things in the sea, is tamed and hath been tamed of mankind: but the tongue can no man tame; it is an unruly evil, full of deadly poison (3:3-8). In swift succession James flashes upon the imaginations of his readers a series of pictures, ranging from zoology to deadly poison. Like a set of vivid carvings they illustrate the complete intractability of the unregenerate tongue.

We can control the great strength of the horse by

means of the bit in his mouth. So also with the ship, a very small rudder enables the captain to steer her. But, the implication seems to be that, whereas a horse or ship is controlled through the one managing the bit or rudder, in the case of man it is the tongue itself that is the arrogant master of body and soul. No wonder James bursts out with this exclamation: "Behold, how great a forest [not "matter," as in the Authorized Version] a little fire kindleth." A chance spark can set a forest fire on its blazing way through thousands of acres of woodland; and James is quick to point the comparison by declaring that the tongue is "a fire . . . defiling the whole body and inflaming the course of nature [literally, "the wheel of birth"], and is set on fire of hell."

The picture is not overdrawn. We have only to recall the havoc wrought in recent years by men, like Lenin or Hitler, possessed of the dangerous gift of eloquence. Whole nations—in fact the majority of the globe—have been set on fire through the demonic power of men with tongues devoted to iniquity.

Next, passing the animal kingdom in review, the writer reminds us that, while there is no creature not tamed by man, the tongue is beyond human power to subdue, intractable and full of deadly poison.

Therewith bless we God, even the Father: and therewith curse we men, which are made after the similitude of God. Out of the same mouth proceedeth blessing and cursing. My brethren, these things ought not so to be. Doth a fountain send forth at the same place sweet water and bitter? Can the fig tree, my brethren, bear olive berries? Either a vine, figs? So can no fountain both yield salt water and fresh (3:9-12). These four verses illustrate the tragic paradox of the tongue, as used both for blessing God and cursing men. Of the objective reality of this paradox, so aptly illustrated by the fountain, fig tree, and vine, there can be no doubt. During World War II, *The New York Times* had an editorial about a famous general in which the statement was made that General — —, who was widely known as a "colorful" personality, was at the same time both "deeply religious and violently profane." What nonsense! What the world calls colorful, the brother of the Lord condemns as a sinful anomaly, exclaiming with shocked emotion: "My brethren, these things ought not so to be!"

There is a curious story of a nobleman of olden times who one day said to his butler: "John, tonight I should like to have the best thing in the world." The hours passed; dinner-time came. The butler set before his master a covered platter. He lifted the silver cover, and there, on the platter, was a cooked tongue. "Good," said the nobleman, "you have done well. But now go and find for me the worst thing in the world." At dinner the next evening, the silver platter was again brought in, the cover lifted, and there was another cooked tongue. Yes, the tongue is both the worst and, if used for God, the best member of the human body.

But how can it be controlled? And is James right when he says, "The tongue can no man tame"? What, in short, is the answer to the problem of the tongue? Some have given a radical reply to questions like these. There was, for example, Armand de Rancé, who founded the order of Trappist monks with their vow of life-long silence. But asceticism is an escape from reality, not a victorious solution of a problem.

James is right; so far as man goes, the tongue *is* incorrigible. Yet as James's divine Brother declared: "The things which are impossible with men are possible with God" (Luke 18:27). The fact is that many Christians through the ages have been given the grace to control their tongues and use them constructively to God's glory. They have not retreated into monasteries, but in the temptations and difficulties of daily living they have been given victory over the unruly member. They have done it, not in their own strength but through submission of mind and heart to the indwelling Christ.

Tongue control? It will never be achieved unless there is first of all heart and mind control. The tongue is the servant of the mind and the emotions. In II Corinthians 10:5, Paul gives us in a single magnificent phrase the key to victory over the tongue: "Bringing into captivity every thought to the obedience of Christ." Whence come our words? They come, of course, from our minds. Antecedent to the word is thought or emotion. Christ only is worthy to have full control of a man's mind. And He who is worthy is also able to do what no man can do for himself. Salvation applies to the whole man. The cleansing of the soul includes also the cleansing of the mind. When any Christian comes to the point of yielding to the Lord—in full sincerity, cost what it may—control of his thought life, the problem of managing his tongue will be solved, provided that such a surrender goes deeper than the intellect and reaches the emotions and the will. For the Bible makes a distinction between mere intellectual knowledge of God and the trust of the heart.

It was our Lord Himself who said: "Out of the abundance of the heart the mouth speaketh" (Matt. 12:34). Words that are truly godly come only from a godly heart. Such a heart is one that is possessed first of all by a deep love for Christ. The heart of the man who really trusts the Lord will express itself in words that are true and edifying.

It is a humbling thing candidly to consider the totality of what comes from our mouths. We are Christians. Therefore, let us say, we sincerely endeavor and generally succeed in eschewing malicious gossip and impure speech. Nor do we use profanity. But are we therefore perfect in respect to our speech? Well, there is a verse in the last book of the Old Testament that will help us answer that question: "Then they that feared the Lord spake often one to another: and the Lord hearkened, and heard it, and a book of remembrance was written before Him for them that feared the Lord, and that thought upon His name" (Mal. 3:16). In the light of these words, we see that it is not enough to avoid overt sins of speech. The Lord looks to His children to use their tongues to His glory in a positive way. "They that feared the Lord spake often one to another." Those words were written of the Jews at one of the lowest ebbs of their national history. Yet there was among them a remnant who really loved the Lord enough to talk frequently about Him.

How much there is that passes for Christian fellowship that is nothing of the kind! We meet with other believers and pass the time in discussing mere trivialities with never a word about Him who should be the very center of our affections.

"But," someone says, "are we never to engage in pleasantries? Surely all our speech cannot be religious." That is quite true. Christianity is a religion that hallows the common things of life; our Lord sanctified by His presence happy, normal human relations, as at the marriage feast at Cana. The danger with us is not that of neglect of this aspect of fellowship; it is the opposite danger of leaving the Lord almost completely out of our speech. Honestly now, how often do we speak of Him? How large a place do His blessings, His goodness, and His wonderful grace have in our everyday conversation? Malachi reminds us of the fact that the Lord not only hears us when we speak of Him but that He also treasures our words and writes them in "a book of remembrance." It is easy to sing in a meeting, "O for a thousand tongues to sing my great Redeemer's praise." Futile wish! We shall never have a thousand tongues. If we had them, we should not know what to do with them—not when the one tongue we have is so strangely silent respecting the Lord who loves us and gave Himself for us.

Who is a wise man and endued with knowledge among you? Let him shew out of a good conversation his works with meekness of wisdom. But if ye have bitter envying and strife in your hearts, glory not, and lie not against the truth. This wisdom descendeth not from above, but is earthly, sensual, devilish. For where envying and strife is, there is confusion and every evil work. But the wisdom that is from above is first pure, then peaceable, gentle, and easy to be intreated, full of mercy and good fruits, without partiality, and without hypocrisy. And the fruit of righteousness is sown in peace of them that make peace (3:13-18). This passage is a transition to the next chapter. Verses 13 and 14 refer back to James's discussion of the tongue, but do so in a general context. The connecting link is the idea of wisdom, introduced by the adjective "wise" in verse 13. Observe the double mention of "wisdom" in the end of this verse and also in verses 15 and 17.

The writer introduces the transition by pointing out that the truly wise man will demonstrate his works through a good manner of life.[1] Essential to such behavior is a controlled tongue. There follows (vs. 14) a contrast, introducing the thought of strife, so powerfully elaborated in the opening verses of the fourth chapter. The spirit of envy and strife is referred to as a special kind of "wisdom," described by three adjectives—"earthly, sensual, devilish." The first and last require no comment, but the second adjective "sensual," better translated "natural," gives us pause in an age which, equating the natural with the right, makes morality subservient to common practice rather than God's moral law. Once more (vs. 16) envy and strife are mentioned, this time as sources of confusion and evil. Certainly one of the most minimized of sins is envy. But the place of envy in the crucifixion unmasks its real nature. As Mark puts it: "The chief priests had delivered him for envy" (Mark 15:10).

From this brief view of the wrong kind of wisdom, James turns to wisdom of the right kind, which he describes as being "from above." He pictures it as the opposite of the earthly wisdom he has just analyzed.

[1] The word used here and in many of the other epistles and translated in the King James Version "conversation," means "manner of life, behavior."

It is, he declares, "first pure." Now in the precedence given to purity there is an abiding lesson. The Christian who today would live in accord with "the wisdom that is from above," can do no better than to ask regarding any doubtful thought, word, or action this plain question: "Is it pure?" If the thing is not pure, it can have no place in Christian life and service. The test is a needed one, especially in an age when purity is being assaulted by a sophistication that degrades some of the most sacred human relations to a lower than animal level.

Not only, however, is the heavenly wisdom pure; it is also, James says, peaceable and gentle, as well as merciful, productive of good works, scrupulously fair and straightforward. Its crowning fruit is peace. Thus with this emphasis upon peace, James completes the transition to his next chapter.

Chapter Six

THE ORIGIN OF STRIFE

FROM WHENCE COME *wars and fightings among you? Come they not hence, even of your lusts that war in your members? Ye lust, and have not: ye kill, and desire to have, and cannot obtain: ye fight and war, yet ye have not, because ye ask not. Ye ask, and receive not, because ye ask amiss, that ye may consume it upon your lusts* (4:1-3). In this chapter James discusses four subjects of great importance: war and its causes; pride and humility; criticism of fellow-believers; and making decisions in disregard of God. The three verses with which the chapter opens are as close to our times as if they appeared in today's newspaper. For they go straight to the heart of the most gigantic of human ills, the problem of war among men and nations. It is a sobering thought that, with all its vaunted scientific and cultural progress, the twentieth century has shed more blood than the millennium preceding it. Thousands of volumes have been written about war. But behind all the economic, geographical, social, religious, and military causes of war which men discuss by millions of words, there lies the root cause set forth by James with the terseness of a telegram.

What, then, is the reason for war? A few years ago, former Chancellor Hutchins of the University of Chicago said war begins in the minds of men. But the writer of this epistle had a deeper insight into humanity. "From whence," he asks, "come wars and fightings among you?" He answers his question by another one: "Come they not hence, even of your lusts that war in your members?" Now it is true that the primary reference here is to strife among those to whom James was writing. That does not alter the fact that, in laying bare the source of quarrels in the Hebrew-Christian communities of the first century, James is also putting his finger upon the cause of war on a national as well as international scale. He knew nothing of psychology as we have it, yet with the timeless pertinence peculiar to Scripture his diagnosis could hardly have been more psychologically up-to-date. "Come they [wars and fightings] not hence, even of your lusts that war in your members?" In other words, James is saying that war begins within men's emotions. Its genesis is not merely on the intellectual level; it goes down into the vast emotional reservoir of life and conduct that underlies the intellectual.[1] It is in this emotional center of man, called by Scripture "the heart," that James says war begins, when the lusts within a man strive together.

It takes only a moment's reflection to realize how true this insight is. From family to nation, war can be traced to tensions inside the individual. Think of the world-wide havoc growing out of the civil war within the heart of an Adolf Hitler. And though a Hitler is fortunately a rarity so far as world-wide influence goes, strife inside the individual is a universal problem, leading to those quarrels that bring sorrow and tragedy in all walks of life. The fact is that man is naturally at war within himself. Only in Christ is this inner conflict fully reconciled, as personality is integrated through faith. Moreover, nations behave like individuals; the lust for possessions of other peoples, the unresolved struggles for power within a country—these too are among the roots of war.

James goes even deeper. There is, he asserts, a way out. "Ye have not, because ye ask not. Ye ask and receive not, because ye ask amiss, that ye may consume it upon your lusts" (vss. 2b, 3). The way out is for men to give up struggling for what is not theirs and to ask God to supply their needs. The initial reference is again

---

[1] This is not to say that the thoughts and emotions of men are in separate compartments. As the study of the human personality shows and as the Bible assumes (cf. phrases like "the thoughts and intents of the heart," Heb. 4:12), emotions and thoughts are inextricably intermingled.

to personal strife inside the community of God's people. As war in general is the extension of individual conflicts, its remedy must go back to peace within the individual. So subtle, however, is the heart of man, that even among God's people prayer is corrupted through unlawful desire. And prayer for something desired *only* for selfish reasons is never prayer that God answers.

Ye adulterers and adulteresses, know ye not the friendship of the world is enmity with God? Whosoever therefore will be a friend of the world is the enemy of God (4:4). The "lusts" just spoken of as corrupting prayer are essentially what Paul and Peter in their epistles call "worldly lusts." So they lead James to a stringent warning against worldliness. "Ye adulterers and adulteresses," he begins, showing at once the strength of his feeling. The best Greek text does not contain the word "adulterers." The omission is consistent with biblical symbolism, wherein Israel is called, in the Old Testament, the wife of Jehovah, and the Church, in the New Testament, the bride of Christ.

Like a spiritual barometer, this verse registers the direction in which a Christian's life is moving. The test may be put thus: "Am I today better friends or worse friends with the world[2] than I was a year ago?" Your answer will show the way you are going spiritually. It

[2] By "world" is meant, not the physical order of nature but the secular, God-forgetting system in which we must live and witness.

is not possible to be at one and the same time out and out for Christ and a close friend of the world. When Christians really grow in the Lord and in His Word, they become less rather than more intimate with the Christ-rejecting system that surrounds them. Charles W. Abel, the great missionary to Papua, once said that Christianity that is really worth anything makes the pagan world progressively less endurable.

What, then, *is* the relationship of the Christian to the world? It may be summed up in seven words: "in the world but not of it." Just as a ship must navigate in the ocean while its inside, engines, cargo, crew, and passengers are kept separate from the ocean, so the Christian, while living in this world, is yet apart from it. When the ocean gets into the ship, it begins to sink; when the world seeps into a Christian life, that life is headed for wreckage.

Do ye think that the Scripture saith in vain, the spirit that dwelleth in us lusteth to envy? (4:5). This is probably the most difficult verse in the epistle. The quotation it makes cannot be exactly identified, nor is the meaning entirely certain. On the other hand, the introductory words are crystal clear. "Do you think," James asks, "that the Scripture saith in vain?" He is speaking to the unfaithful believers whom he has just called "adulteresses" because of their worldly compromise. In the larger application, however, the question sounds in the ears of all men everywhere. "Do you think that the Scripture speaks in vain?" "Well," we may ask ourselves, "do we?" Do we think the Bible ever speaks in an empty, vague way (the meaning of "vain")? The trouble is that, while most Christians would answer with an emphatic "No," the honest reply, according to the practice of many a life, must be "Yes." Whenever a decision is faced in self-will, whenever God's Word is read thoughtlessly, whenever a sermon true to the Bible is shrugged off, then Scripture is speaking "in vain." The whole level of life in our churches would be different, were Christians really to take the whole Word of God seriously.

When we come to the second part of the verse, we meet two difficulties: the source of the quotation, and its meaning. Of the source of the quotation, it must be said that the words given here appear nowhere in the Old Testament. "The Scripture" referred to is not a specific quotation, but perhaps some larger portion, the gist of which is here summarized. And what do the words, "the spirit that dwelleth in us lusteth to envy" mean? Of various suggested interpretations the most satisfactory is that of Dean Alford, whose paraphrase reads like this: "The Spirit God made to dwell in us earnestly desires us for His own."[3] This reading sup-

[3] Cf. *The Greek Testament,* by Henry Alford. The more common interpretation sees *pneuma* ("spirit") as referring to man's spirit, thus making the words a warning against the innate envy of the unregenerate heart. If this is correct, then the reference may be to such passages as Genesis 6:5; 8:21; and Numbers 11:29. But if we join Dean Alford

plements the warning of verse 4 against spiritual unfaithfulness by stressing the fact that the Holy Spirit desires complete possession of the believer whom He indwells. And indeed, a life given to worldly compromise is robbing the Spirit of God of a portion of His rightful possession. Yet this is just what the carnal believer does when he sets up worldly idols in a heart that, as the temple of God, belongs to the Holy Spirit.

---

in making *pneuma* refer to the Holy Spirit, then the reference may be to Exodus 20:3-5; Galatians 5:7; and Matthew 6:24. The writer feels that this is probably the correct exegesis, because it best fits the context.

Chapter Seven

PRIDE AND SECULARISM

BUT HE GIVETH *more grace. Wherefore He saith, God resisteth the proud, but giveth grace unto the humble. Submit yourselves therefore to God. Resist the devil, and he will flee from you. Draw nigh to God, and He will draw nigh to you. Cleanse your hands, ye sinners; and purify your hearts ye double minded. Be afflicted, and mourn, and weep: let your laughter be turned to mourning, and your joy to heaviness. Humble yourselves in the sight of the Lord, and He shall lift you up* (4:6-10). James now makes a wonderfully reassuring statement: "But He giveth," he writes, "more grace," meaning by "He" none other than God, whose Spirit yearns to have us for His own. The pull of the world may be great, but greater is the grace of Him who has overcome the world. Whereupon the apostle declares: "God resisteth the proud, but giveth grace to the humble."

From worldly compromise to pride—the transition is a logical one; for a leading motive of worldliness is surely pride. Let us pause, therefore, at this mention of "the proud," as we observe that, whatever else may be said of pride, it is everlastingly true that God is against it. Men may not consider pride a very serious matter. Yet in belittling it, they presume to reverse the divine evaluation of this sin. In Solomon's list of the seven things God hates, pride stands first.[1] The sin through which Satan fell, it is at one and the same time the worst and the most lightly regarded of sins. In fact, there are even those, and not all of them are unbelievers, who take a certain satisfaction in pride. But James bluntly says that God is against it. Let whoever will be proud; but let him also realize once and for all that, in so far as he is proud, none other than the living God is resisting him.

We look, then, at this most underrated of sins in its true light. What is pride? It is the sin that, arrogating to self the credit belonging to God alone, cheats Him of the honor due His name. In wicked self-sufficiency, it by-passes the Sovereign of heaven and earth and presumes to act in wilful independence. It is the very spirit of secularism, the leading characteristic of this God-forgetting age in which we live.

Nor are Christians immune to the contagion of this sin. Whenever we yield to the desire to live our own

[1] Proverbs 6:16-19.

lives in our own way, forgetting that we are not our own but Christ's, bought with the price of His precious blood; whenever we make decisions in our own wisdom apart from a prayerful seeking of the will of God; whenever we glorify self and self-achievement, ignoring the fact that all we are and have is from the Lord; then we are guilty of pride. By the same token God is against us in all His mighty power.

The opposite of pride is humility, and James quickly turns to it, reminding us that God's grace abounds toward the humble. There follows a brief passage (vss. 7-10), wherein this virtue is discussed in vivid and practical words. How are we to overcome pride? By being humble. But how to be humble? James leaves us in no doubt about this all-important matter. Through a swift succesion of some half-dozen exhortations, he gives the practical answer to pride.

"Submit yourselves therefore to God." The essence of pride being self-sufficiency, unconditional surrender to God is its antidote. "Resist the devil, and he will flee from you." The author of pride being Satan, the surrendered Christian is part of a perpetual resistance movement. In his hand are two weapons: "the sword of the Spirit" and "all prayer" (Eph. 6:17, 18). "Draw nigh to God, and He will draw nigh to you." The words of the old hymn, "Nearer my God to Thee," may well be the motto for the believer who would depart from pride. And as he does draw near, he finds that, like the father in the parable of the prodigal, God is already near him. "Cleanse your hands, ye sinners and purify your hearts, ye double-minded."[2] God demands purity of those who would come close to Him. It is not enough, therefore, to cleanse the hands, i.e., the outward life. This, though essential, must be accompanied by a pure heart. Only the blood of Christ can cleanse the sinner's heart. "Be afflicted, and mourn, and weep: let your laughter be turned to mourning and your joy to heaviness." Behind this exhortation there sound the words of James's divine Brother in His Sermon on the Mount: "Blessed are they that mourn . . ."[3] It is not that laughter and joy are wrong; on the contrary, joy is the birthright of believers. The trouble is that we are so prone to rejoice in the wrong things. Therefore, the worldly lusts that rejoice the unregenerate nature ought to cause Christians repentant sorrow. "Humble yourselves in the sight of the Lord, and He shall lift you up." True exaltation of heart and life comes only from self-abasement before the Lord. Nothing but clear-sighted apprehension of our utter unworthiness apart from Christ can lead to true humility.

Humility. How little it is known and practised in our present-day Christianity! So subtle is our human nature that humility is unattainable, apart from the

---

[2] Literally "two-souled." James uses again the adjective that appears in 1:8.

[3] Matthew 5:4.

grace of God. A homely anecdote will illustrate the fact. One day a Christian farmer, troubled by the sin of pride, went to a little shed in a remote corner of his fields, where he lay in the dust all day, abasing himself before God. Finally he got up and walked homeward. As he walked along in the sunset light suddenly the thought came: "After all, there are few, if any, other men in this county who have lain in the dust all day and gotten as humble as I." Now this proud thought may not have destroyed his humility, provided that his humility was sincere and provided that he instantly repudiated the thought. It did show, however, how incorrigible the natural heart is and how no amount of pious exertion can overcome it. For the final answer to pride lies quite outside ourselves. It lies in our apprehension of what Christ did upon the cross. We may set it down as a principle that no one who really knows the meaning of Calvary—not as a spectacle of the past but as a living reality of what the Son of God suffered for him—will continue to live in pride. This being the case, it must be said that the reason why Christians succumb to the sin of pride is because they have allowed Calvary, once they have enjoyed its benefit, to become unreal to them. When all is said and done, we have in the words of Isaac Watts the final remedy for pride:

> When I survey the wondrous cross
> On which the Prince of glory died,

My richest gain I count but loss
And pour contempt on all my pride.

Speak not evil one of another, brethren. He that speaketh evil of his brother, and judgeth his brother, speaketh evil of the law, and judgeth the law: but if thou judge the law, thou art not a doer of the law, but a judge. There is one lawgiver, who is able to save and to destroy: who art thou that judgest another? (4:11, 12). Here James sounds again one of the major notes of his epistle. In the opening chapter,[4] he touched for the first time upon control of the tongue; in the third chapter,[5] he treated this subject at length; and now he returns to it through showing the spiritual implications of un-Christian criticism of the brethren. To do this, he says, is tantamount to sitting in judgment upon the law. By "the law," James means "the royal law"[6] or "the law of liberty"[7] which is the same thing as Christ's law of love.[8] Therefore, to slander the Lord's children is to place oneself in contempt of the law of Christ by presuming, as it were, to judge it. Solemnly, James reminds those who do this that behind the law of love there is the Lawgiver, who holds the power of life and death. Once more, the reader sensitive to the harmony of Scripture hears an echo of the Sermon on the Mount with its searching warning, "Judge not that ye be not

[4] 1:19, 26.
[5] 3:1-12.
[6] 2:8.
[7] 1:25.
[8] 2:8.

judged," followed by the striking figure of the mote and the beam.[9]

Go to now, ye that say, Today or tomorrow we will go into such a city, and continue there a year, and buy and sell, and get gain: whereas ye know not what shall be on the morrow. For what is your life? It is even a vapour, that appeareth for a little time, and then vanisheth away. For that ye ought to say, If the Lord will, we shall live, and do this, or that. But now ye rejoice in your boastings: all such rejoicing is evil. Therefore to him that knoweth to do good, and doeth it not, to him it is sin (4:13-17). Behind many of James's words there are pictures. One sees here the assured man of affairs. "In the morning," he says, "I will be moving my office to another city, where for a year I will be doing business at a large profit." But he takes no thought of Him who alone controls human destiny. That such planning is simply another manifestation of God-forgetting pride is clear from verse 16: "But now ye rejoice in your boastings: all such rejoicing is evil."

As a corrective, James sets before his readers the transitoriness of human life, comparing it to vapor. All who have seen the evanescent clouds swirling round the mountain heights, the quiet mist rising from the waters of a still lake in the pre-dawn hours, or the silent fog shrouding a sea-coast village, will understand the aptness of the figure. In view, then, of the uncer-

[9] Matthew 7:1-5.

tainty of life which depends moment by moment upon the drawing of breath into our lungs, we should, James is telling us, have a constant regard for God's over-ruling providence. Far better than the rash assurance of counting on what we are going to do in a year, or even tomorrow, we should qualify all our planning with a reverent, "If the Lord will." The custom of using "D.V."[10] in friendly and even business correspondence has fallen pretty much into the discard. There is, of course, no magic in the merely traditional use of such an expression. But its thoughtful use is both honoring to the Lord and a testimony to the secularist who makes plans in disregard of God. A truly Christian attitude toward life is one that recognizes Him at all times and in all things. As Dr. J. Stuart Holden put it, "Live a moment at a time and that moment with God."

Finally, lest there be the slightest doubt about the real nature of going ahead without proper deference to God's will, James sums up by declaring that to know the good and not to do it is sin. The verse has wide implications. For one thing, it shows the folly of all pretensions to sinless perfection. In view of this simple declaration, what honest man would dare claim sinlessness? Think of it! To leave unheeded any prompting of the Spirit to prayer; not to speak a word of witness when opportunity affords; to fail to give as liberally as

[10] "D.V." is an abbreviation for the Latin, *Deo volente,* meaning "The Lord willing."

God would have; to keep silent when truth should be defended; not to meditate upon the things of the Lord when such meditation would please Him; or to allow the things of earth to divert the mind from Him in time of worship; in short, not to love the Lord our God with *all* our heart and soul and mind—all these are sin. In the light of such criteria, the claim to sinless perfection is nothing short of impious nonsense. Far better to acknowledge our constant falling short and to find our acceptance with God only through the righteousness of Him who alone was sinless, than to delude ourselves with claiming a perfection no man can possibly attain.

Chapter Eight

THE PERIL OF UNSANCTIFIED RICHES

GO TO NOW, *ye rich men, weep and howl for your miseries that shall come upon you. Your riches are corrupted, and your garments are motheaten. Your gold and silver is cankered, and the rust of them shall be a witness against you, and shall eat your flesh as it were fire. Ye have heaped treasure together for the last days. Behold, the hire of the labourers who have reaped down your fields, which is of you kept back by fraud, crieth; and the cries of them which have reaped are entered into the ears of the Lord of sabaoth. Ye have lived in pleasure on the earth, and been wanton; ye have nourished your hearts, as in a day of slaughter. Ye have condemned and killed the just; and he doth not resist you* (5:1-6). These verses, like the beginning of the second chapter, deal with the rich. However, the warning against respect of persons in chapter 2 is addressed to those within the Christian congregation, while here it is the ungodly rich who are in view. The passage flames with indignation, reflecting the sterner side of Christ's teaching. For there were times when James's divine Brother spoke in burning words against the sins of the privileged. Our Lord was Prophet as well as Saviour. Like Amos and Jeremiah, He denounced evil and called for righteousness. If we remember that James also stands in this succession, we shall be helped to understand his deep concern for matters of social justice that some Christians carelessly forget.

Observe the vigor of his words, as James describes the retribution surely to overtake the oppressing rich. "Go along now, you plutocrats," he is saying, "you will be howling for fair when you get the misery that is coming to you." Then he pictures an oriental piling up of wealth—costly garments and heaps of silver and golden objects—not only decaying in themselves but also eating into the lives of their ungodly possessors. So these treasures have been accumulated for "the last days." While this phrase probably points to the fall of Jerusalem in A.D. 70, when about a million Jews, rich and poor alike, perished in one of the most awful sieges in history, it may also be thought of as looking forward to the end time, called elsewhere in the New Testament, "the last days."[1]

Let us be sure that we understand James. He is not denouncing wealth *per se*. By itself, money, along with

[1] Cf., for example, II Timothy 3:1; II Peter 3:3.

other legitimate forms of riches, is morally neutral. It is the abuse of money that corrodes men's lives. Properly used, great wealth can be a means of blessing; in consecrated hands, it can be employed for the upbuilding of the work of God. But once let money become the master instead of remaining the servant of man, and the door is open for all sorts of oppression and exploitation.

It is these abuses that the apostle is excoriating. In doing so, he raises his voice against a kind of injustice about which the Church has too often been silent. "Look out!" he exclaims. "The starvation wages of the workers in your fields,[2] whom you have cheated, cry aloud your injustice; the complaint of the laborers you have been exploiting has reached the ears of the Lord of hosts Himself. You have," he goes on, "been indulging yourselves by living in the lap of luxury; but your very self-indulgence is preparing your wicked hearts for judgment as cattle are fattened for slaughter." And then, pointing to what the abuses he has been describing can lead, he declares: "You have condemned and killed the just; and he doth not resist you."

Who is "the just"[3] of whom James speaks? Like Stephen, in his defense,[4] the apostle may have been thinking of the succession of Old Testament prophets.

---

[2] The figure is an agricultural one, but had James been writing in our time, he might have mentioned such things as mines and industrial plants.

[3] The word means "righteous."

[4] Acts 7:52.

He also may have had in mind the Lord Jesus, called by Stephen in the same context "The Just One."[5] It is interesting, too, that the words may be an unconscious prophecy of James's own end. We remember that he himself was known as "the just" and recall that, according to tradition, he was martyred. Be that as it may, the killing of "the just" is the logical outcome of that cynical unconcern for their fellowmen, so characteristic of the arrogant rich.

Let us not forget, moreover, that what James has been saying about unconsecrated riches is just as applicable in this day as in the first century. Our own America, the richest nation on earth, needs to take it to heart. A nation that spends almost twice as much for television sets as it gives to religious organizations, that spends seven times as much on automobiles as it gives to religion—has not learned the right use of wealth. Nor would the record be proportionately much better for the other so-called "Christian" countries. No wonder the world seethes with unrest.

The answer? Not ungodly communism which substitutes for the selfishness of professing Christendom a more callous disregard of human rights than has ever been seen before this twentieth century. No, the answer is the outright Christian submission of all we possess—money included—to God, looking to Him to guide in its use. And if someone objects that this cannot be

[5] Acts 7:52.

expected of unbelievers, let us not argue the matter. Let us rather see to it that we who know the Lord are devoted to Him in all things, and that our relations with our fellowmen are in all respects such as He would approve. For our sovereign God is concerned with injustice wherever it is practised, either by the believer or the unbeliever.

Chapter Nine

PATIENCE AND THE LORD'S RETURN

BE PATIENT THEREFORE, *brethren, unto the coming of the Lord. Behold, the husbandman waiteth for the precious fruit of the earth, and hath long patience for it, until he receive the early and latter rain. Be ye also patient; stablish your hearts: for the coming of the Lord draweth nigh. Grudge not one against another, brethren, lest ye be condemned: behold, the judge standeth before the door. Take, my brethren, the prophets, who have spoken in the name of the Lord, for an example of suffering affliction, and of patience. Behold, we count them happy which endure. Ye have heard of the patience of Job, and have seen the end of the Lord; that the Lord is very pitiful, and of tender mercy* (5:7-11). With the mention of "patience," our thoughts are again directed backward—this time to the opening of the epistle, where James stresses this virtue.[1] Now he re-

[1] 1:3, 12.

verts to patience and develops it at some length, relating it to the return of the Lord and illustrating it from nature and from the experience of the prophets.

The connection is logical. Turning from the ungodly rich, the apostle addresses his Christian readers, some of whom may well have suffered the oppression he has been denouncing, and exhorts them to be patient. The incentive for endurance of affliction is "the coming[2] of the Lord." In verse 8, the same thought recurs in slightly different form: "Be ye also patient; stablish your hearts: for the coming of the Lord draweth nigh." And in verse 9, there is a third allusion to the second coming in the statement: "Behold, the judge standeth before the door." Thus does James add his voice to the unanimous testimony of the New Testament authors to the great truth of Christ's return. To be sure, he does not treat the subject at length. He simply declares it as an inescapable fact, emphasizing, as he does so, its imminence.

Some have misunderstood the mention in verse 7 of "the early and latter rain." It is not sound exegesis to make the "latter rain" mean another outpouring of the Spirit subsequent to Pentecost, thought by those who hold this view to be "the early rain." To do this is to read into James's words something that is not there. In reality the two rains refer simply to the patience of the

[2] Here and in verse 8 James uses *parousia,* the word used by Paul (I Thess. 4:15) of the Rapture (Christ's coming for His Church).

farmer in Palestine as he awaits the May and October rains characteristic of that land.

There follows a warning regarding a spirit of complaint[3] against fellow-Christians. Doubtless James has in mind the kind of impatience that leads to unbrotherly criticism. Once more, the return of the Lord is alluded to, this time in its judgment aspect, as James declares, "Behold, the judge standeth before the door" (vs. 9b). It is a solemn picture of the inevitable fact of human accountability to the living God. As James dramatically puts it, before the door of every man's life the Judge of all the earth is standing. When He returns, He will open the door and come through to reckon with man. And if He does not return in our lifetime, we shall still have to meet Him as, like the billions of human beings who have preceded us, we go through the door of death at the other side of which the Judge is waiting. Either way, the fact is inescapable.

It is a shallow kind of Christianity that, seeing only God's grace in the Gospel, forgets inevitable judgment. For the regenerate, judgment respecting the eternal destiny of the soul is past; on Calvary Christ paid the price of the believer's sin. Yet for the regenerate, too, the Judge awaits, because the New Testament teaches that "we must all appear before the judgment seat of Christ; that every one may receive the things done in his own body, according to that he hath done, whether

[3] The word translated "grudge" means "complain."

it be good or bad."[4] This judgment of the believer pertains to his works; it represents an accounting for the stewardship of his whole life—his talents, money, and time. And while no redeemed soul will lose his salvation, there will be many who will suffer shame as they lose the heavenly rewards they might have had. A proper understanding of the inescapability of the believer's judgment before the Lord Jesus Christ is the scriptural remedy for the careless living that enfeebles many a church today.

Before leaving the subject of patience, James points to the prophet as an example of endurance under affliction. "Behold, we count them happy which endure" (vs. 11 is reminiscent of the beatitude in the twelfth verse of chapter 1. Of special interest is the reference to Job (vs. 11b), which is the source of the proverbial expression, "the patience of Job." When James speaks of "the end of the Lord," he means the way in which God finally resolved Job's difficulties by revealing His greatness and giving His sorely tried servant material blessings comparable to those he had lost.

But above all things, my brethren, swear not, neither by heaven, neither by the earth, neither by any other oath: but let your yea be yea; and your nay, nay; lest ye fall into condemnation. Is any among you afflicted? let him pray. Is any merry? Let him sing plasms (5:12,

[4] II Corinthians 5:10. Cf. also I Corinthians 3:11-15.

13). The last reference in the epistle to the believer's speech, this is also the final allusion to the Sermon on the Mount. Its similarity to the teaching of our Lord (Matt. 5:33-37)[5] is unmistakable. Rash vows were common among the first century Jews, such swearing being an oral response to deep emotion like extreme joy. Seeing the folly of irresponsible oath-taking, James joins the Lord Jesus in his advocacy of an unadorned "Yes" and "No" in place of elaborate and impious vows. As the outlet of strong feeling, he tersely advises prayer in case of affliction and the singing of psalms in case of joy.

[5] "Again, ye have heard that it hath been said by them of old time, Thou shalt not forswear thyself, but shalt perform unto the Lord thine oaths; but I say unto you, Swear not at all; neither by heaven; for it is God's throne: nor by the earth; for it is His footstool: neither by Jerusalem; for it is the city of the great King. Neither shalt thou swear by thy head, because thou canst not make one hair white or black. But let your communication be, Yea, yea; Nay, nay; for whatsoever is more than these cometh of evil" (Matthew 5:33-37).

Chapter Ten

HEALING AND PRAYER

IS ANY SICK *among you? Let him call for the elders of the church, and let them pray over him, anointing him with oil in the name of the Lord: and the prayer of faith shall save the sick, and the Lord shall raise him up; and if he have committed sins, they shall be forgiven him. Confess your faults one to another, and pray one for another that ye may be healed* (5:14-16a). Few passages in Scripture have been more extensively misinterpreted and misunderstood than these three verses. Roman Catholicism has distorted their meaning; Pentecostalism and other faith-healing sects have done likewise. That verse 14 should be used as a proof text for the "sacrament" of extreme unction is a revelation of Romish misuse of Scripture. It is as plain as day that the anointing with oil here described is for the physical restoration of the sick (vs. 15); but extreme unction is administered before death. Nor is Rome any more logical in using the confession here spoken of to bolster the "sacrament" of auricular confession to a priest, when James says to Christians in general, "Confess your faults [sins] one to another." As Luther exclaimed, "A strange confessor! His name is One Another."

Likewise unsound is the application of this passage by Pentecostal sects in widely heralded "Healing Campaigns." Through much publicity and advertising the sick are brought to the meetings, whereas James says that the sick man is to call the elders of the church to come to him. The resemblance of such use of these verses to what James was talking about is superficial. Whatever else it was, the scene James described was intimate and personal, not a public display.

But granted that Romanism and Pentecostalism are wrong in their applications of this passage, what is its correct interpretation?

There are some who point out that oil was one of the commonest of ancient remedies. Galen, the famous Greek physician, mentions it; Pliny and Philo refer to it as a therapeutic agent; and it was used in Herod's last illness. In our Lord's parable, the good Samaritan treated the traveler's wounds with oil and wine. On the basis of such evidence, the inference is drawn that James is counseling the use of medical means along with prayer. The analogy from ancient medicine is enlightening. But to accept it as the full answer to the problem of the passage entails making mere oil the panacea for every form of illness, an obvious absurdity.

More satisfactory than the foregoing interpretation is the common sense procedure—always the basic method in Bible study—of seeing exactly what the text says. For when we understand the primary meaning of Scripture in its historical setting, we have the essential key to its understanding. Earlier in our study of the epistle we have used this key, as in the beginning of chapter 2, where we saw that in describing the problem of snobbery in church James was painting a picture from the life of his time. So in this case he is giving us a description of the actual practice in the first-century church. There is the sick man. He sends for the elders of the church to visit him. They respond to the emergency call. They "pray over him [the words show us the elders bending over the sick man's bed], anointing him with oil in the name of the Lord." There can be no question that James is portraying what he has seen.

But questions arise. Is this scene, so vividly described by James, to be the pattern for all subsequent Christian procedure in case of sickness? And, to be even more specific, is the use of oil normative for the treatment of illness among believers? In short, is James describing a sacramental act, the performance of which has a particular virtue? We think not.

Consider the use of oil in Scripture. In the old dispensation it was prominent. But in the New Testament, very little is said of it. In fact, its significant mention in Mark 6:13 occurs in a passage descriptive of the precrucifixion ministry of the disciples, as they went about among the Jews, preaching repentance and proclaiming the kingdom. Following the crucifixion and resurrection, however, there is little mention of oil. It does not appear in The Acts, is completely absent from the Pauline epistles, and, of the other epistolary writers James alone[1] speaks of it. Why he does so is plain enough. It may well be that the church at Jerusalem, with its distinctively Jewish tradition, retained for a time a traditional practice of this kind. Seen in this light, the procedure James describes is obviously not binding upon future generations of Christians. *But the principle behind it* is *binding.* Oil, in Scripture, is the symbol of the Holy Spirit. With the descent of the Spirit at Pentecost, the need for the symbol passed. The Comforter, the antitype of the oil, had come. Indwelling the believer, guiding the Church, He was a present and continuing reality.

What, then, is the abiding lesson of the passage? Simply this. In the case of sickness among Christians, prayer in the Holy Spirit is essential. Not that medical means are to be despised. It is not a matter of *either* prayer *or* medicine but of *both* prayer *and* medicine. For Christians, it is God *and* medicine, with God *first.*

In few areas of life is there more need for balance

[1] The seeming exception in Hebrews 1:9 is a quotation from Psalm 45.

than in the matter of healing. Because sickness is such a personal and universal thing, because much of it is emotional and psychological rather than simply physical, because some of it is directly related to sin, the tendency to extremes is always present. But the New Testament, properly understood—i.e., taken in its entirety—does not go to extremes. It does not make *all* sickness the result of specific, personal sin,[2] it does not repudiate the use of medical means,[3] yet it constantly enjoins prayer when illness comes. That prayer—earnest, united prayer in the power of the Holy Spirit—has been answered unto the recovery of the sick is undeniable. Countless Christians know, not theoretically but experientially, the efficacy of prayer in time of grave illness. Even unbelieving physicians admit instances when recovery, though medically impossible, came because of prayer. Yes, James is right: "The prayer of faith shall save the sick." (Observe that he does not say: "The anointing oil shall save the sick.")

But what of the next statement? "And if he [the sick man] have committed sins, they shall be forgiven him." Several explanations come to mind. In the first place, the reference may be to illness directly linked to sin,

---

[2] Consider the case of Epaphroditus who "was sick nigh unto death . . . for the work of Christ" (Phil. 2:25-30).

[3] Paul, recognizing the weak stomach of his young colleague Timothy, prescribed for him the medicinal use of wine (I Tim. 5:23). It is significant also that Luke, the traveling companion of Paul, was a physician.

in which case the restoration would be spiritual as well as physical. But by no means all illness comes from personal sin. Therefore, the words must have another meaning, relating, perhaps, as some have suggested, to sins against the brethren which, now that the sick brother is well again, will be forgiven by those he has wronged. Or again, the words may be taken broadly to mean simply that the Lord, who graciously heals the ills of the body, will not fail to forgive the maladies of the soul.

"Confess your faults one to another, and pray one for another that ye may be healed" (vs. 16a). Here mutual confession among Christians, which is quite a different matter from confession to a priest, is enjoined. Some have tried to limit such confession to things of minor import because the Authorized Version speaks of "faults." The Greek word, translated "faults," is *harmartias,* which is the regular New Testament word for "sins." Plainly, James is reminding us of one of the less easy implications of Christian living.

There are some who advocate public confession of personal, intimate sins. But James's words by no means require this. In general, the character of the sin determines the manner of confession. There are sins in which an individual is wronged; let them be confessed to that individual. Others affect a group, a church, for example; they should be confessed to the group. Still others are sins against God alone, and they should be confessed only to Him. To be sure, all sins are against God and therefore they should all be confessed to God, even though some sins against men need to be confessed to men as well.

Confession is a powerful deterrent to sin. The Christian who has told a lie and, convicted of his transgression, has made it right with the one he has deceived, will find it harder to tamper with the truth in the future. The believer who, having wronged his brethren, tells them with repentance what he has done, will be more careful of his actions. Yes, confession is difficult. In that very fact lies its power for good. Surely one of the reasons why some believers are living on a level far below the high doctrine they profess is that the obligation of confession is so comparatively neglected in our present-day Christianity.

Turning back to the context, we see that confession does not stand alone. It is linked with prayer—"pray for one another," James continues—and it is followed by a result—"that ye may be healed." The latter clause raises questions. Is physical healing meant? Or is James speaking of forgiveness in the sense of healing of the soul. There is, of course, a connection between prayerful confession and forgiveness. But to apply these words exclusively to the soul is to ignore their plain meaning. After all, unconfessed sin and unanswered prayer go together. Known sin, hidden and not repented of, wrongs not made right—these are hindrances to prevailing prayer. But, if they are confessed and rectified, and fellowship with God and the brethren is re-established, then prayer for healing may well be answered. Moreover, the unburdening of a troubled heart may lead to physical relief, so intimately are body and soul united. The consciousness of sins forgiven and the peace of a clear conscience have a healing effect upon the whole human organism.

The effectual fervent prayer of a righteous man availeth much. Elias was a man subject to like passions as we are, and he prayed earnestly that it might not rain: and it rained not on the earth by the space of three years and six months. And he prayed again, and the heaven gave rain, and the earth brought forth her fruit (5:16b-18). James now directs our attention to prayer, as he states a principle and then illustrates it. Prayer and the character of the pray-er cannot be separated. It is the "righteous" man of Elijah-like character who prays most effectively. Those who live nearest the Lord are most mighty in prayer. Who of us has not, in time of stress, asked some godly friend to pray? Elijah was such a man, though "subject to like passions as we are," James adds, lest we think Elijah impossibly above us. Then, referring to the story in I Kings,[4] he tells how the prophet's prayers, first for drought and then for rain, were answered.

Yes, "the effectual fervent prayer of a righteous man

[4] I Kings 17:1 and 18:42.

availeth much." But is it always answered? To be specific, does "the prayer of faith" heal the sick in every case? When we answer questions like these negatively, as we must, then we are face to face with the mystery of prayer. On the one hand, we know that it avails much; we know that God answers it. On the other hand, there are times when, while praying just as earnestly, with just as sincere faith, with heart and conscience void of offense toward God and man, we do not have the longed-for answer.

God heals the sick through prayer—but not always; otherwise ailing Christians for whom prayer is continually made would never die. God sends rain in answer to Elijah-like prayer, but not in every case. There is ever the underlying factor of His sovereign will. The Almighty is not our servant to be summoned to do everything we want Him to do. All prayer is conditional. Though James does not set forth its conditions, they are clearly stated elsewhere in the New Testament. A spirit of forgiveness, an attitude of abiding in Christ and having His Word abide in us, a trusting heart, a humble submission to God's will—these are the conditions of true prayer. When they are met, there will always be an answer. More than that, it will always be the right answer, even though it may not in every case correspond with our own desire. For the highest we can possibly seek in every circumstance is to have the will of God done in us, whether by life or by death.

Brethren, if any of you do err from the truth, and one convert him, let him know that he which converteth the sinner from the error of his way shall save a soul from death, and shall hide a multitude of sins (5:19,20). With this appeal, James concludes. It is an abrupt ending, quite different from the close of any of the other epistles, yet fully in keeping with the plain-spoken James. The note it strikes is the vital one of evangelism. As Dr. Robert Scott said: "And so James concludes, as if saying that if but one soul were won to Christ by his Epistle he would be well repaid and that he would have every Christian feel this, even as he himself felt it." We see, therefore, that a burden for souls goes hand in hand with consistent Christian living.

The final verse—"Let him know that he which converteth the sinner from the error of his way shall save a soul from death, and shall hide a multitude of sins"—has, like much else in the epistle, been misunderstood. Its meaning, however, is plain. James is not saying that the Christian who is used of God for the conversion of another will thereby cover a multitude of his own sins. Evangelism is a great and good work, but to think of it as covering one's own personal sins is a perversion of the Gospel. There is only one covering for sins, and that is the atoning blood of the Lord

Jesus Christ. Actually James is saying that the believer who leads even one sinner to Christ is being used to cover the multitudinous sins of the one who has been converted. The emphasis is a completely unselfish one, beautifully characteristic of the apostle of applied Christianity, whose letter so uniquely reflects the mind of the Lord Jesus.

THE END